To Jane,
With Compliments
David Mich
March 24, 2000

TELLING THE STORY

Telling the Story

Black Pentecostals in the Church of God

DAVID MICHEL

PATHWAY PRESS

Unless otherwise indicated, Scripture quotations are from the King James Version of the Bible.

Book Editor: Wanda Griffith
Editorial Assistant: Tammy Hatfield
Inside Layout: Mark Shuler
Copy Editor: Cresta Shawver

Library of Congress Card Catalogue Number: 99-068978

ISBN: 0-87148-946-5

Copyright © 2000 by Pathway Press

Cleveland, Tennessee 37311

All Rights Reserved

Printed in the United States of America

Dedication

This book is dedicated to:

- My loving parents, the Reverend and Mrs. Samuel Michel, who understood my dreams and contributed sacrificially to my education
- The memory of the early black pioneer ministers who are now enjoying their eternal rest
- Black ministers who are following the tradition of their fathers
- The international black constituency
- The young people, who will be inspired by this book
- All who love and appreciate the ministry of the black Church of God

Contents

Foreword 9
Acknowledgments 11
Introduction 15

PART 1: MAJOR EVENTS IN THE BLACK CHURCH ... 17

1. The Early Beginnings 1884-1922 19
2. Expanded Autonomy 1923-1966 27
3. The Historic Black Church of God 37
4. Evangelism in the Black Church 45
5. The New Testament Church of God 57
6. Ethnic Growth 67
7. Jamaican and Haitian Congregations 75

PART 2: BIOLOGICAL PROFILES 87

8. Leadership in the Black Church 89
9. More Outstanding Evangelists 101
10. Social Ministry and Education 119
11. Missions in the Black Church 127
12. The Modern Period 1967-Present 139

Conclusion 149
Chronology of Important Events 153
Notes 159

Foreword

The importance of the Pentecostal Movement and its impact on the universal church has long been recognized by the illiterate and unschooled in society. Despite its source and tendencies toward the poor and abandoned, the factor of race has played, and continues to play, a major discriminatory role in how the story is told in the United States.

While the events of Azusa Street are well known and carefully chronicled in scholastic circles, and at times even treated a consequence of the Evangelical Movement, little attention has been paid to its manifestations among African-American, Caribbean, Latin and African peoples. Indeed the stories, when written or told for the wider arena, are more often one-sided and biased. When written or told, it is often in odious comparison with prophetic or spirit movements in anthropological or sociological studies or with emphasis on the social and political consequences as in Allende's Chile.

Only recently has Pentecostalism been taken seriously on the world stage. The monumental and defining studies by Hollenweger from Europe and in the United States, and the studies and publications of Dayton, Robeck and others have made sterling contributions to academia. Perhaps Pentecostalism may have remained in the background had there not been three events that catapulted the Movement to the forefront. The first is the Charismatic Movement in mainline churches, which enabled their membership to identify with Pentecostals and give a higher social profile to the Movement. Second is the publication of *Tongues of Fire*, by the celebrated Harvey Cox, of "Secular City" fame who sees Pentecostalism as the future church. The third event was the concern of Pope John Paul II at the decimation of the Roman Church in Latin America because of defections to Pentecostal churches.

Telling the Story is seen within this wider context. Its concern to tell the unknown stories of African-American preachers and their Caribbean counterparts is welcomed as an educational tool to set the record straight for current and future generations. It brings to the forefront, not only the story of a minority (blacks in the Church of God), but also that of a minority within a minority—the Church of God in Christ. As a member of the Church of God, David Michel combines academic insight with evangelical passion. This makes for good reading.

I pray that this book will inspire others to tell other untold stories of the Pentecostal Movement—especially those of African descent in the United States, in the Caribbean, and in Africa, Asia and Europe.

—Dr. Horace O. Russell
Professor of Historical Theology and Dean of Chapel
Eastern Baptist Theological Seminary

Acknowledgments

For many years, I waited for someone to write the story of blacks in the Church of God. When it finally dawned on me that such a book might never be written, I finally committed to write it, paying the price and researching countless dusty documents.

This book provides only a general survey of the life of the black church. Therefore, it should not be read as a social history. The term *black,* as used in the title, should be understood in a broad sense, designating people of African descent. Because of research constraints, my focus has been limited to African-Americans and West Indians living in North America and England. It is my hope that others will catch the vision and explore uncovered areas of the black work, especially in Africa and the West Indies.

It is impossible to thank everyone who contributed in one way or another to this book. I must mention the following people who have shaped my understanding of church history: Dr. Eric Ohlmann, academic dean and professor of Christian heritage, Eastern Baptist Theological Seminary, who introduced me to the complexities of church history as a science; Dr. Horace O. Russell, professor of historical theology, Eastern Baptist Theological Seminary, who painted the beauty of the black church; David G. Roebuck, Church of God Theological Seminary, for a scholarly survey of Church of God history; and Dr. Grant McClung who inspired me.

The Reverends Jean and Marie Vincent have served for the last 15 years as my spiritual advisors. I am grateful to them for nurturing in me the importance of trusting God. May they remember that I will always cherish their friendship and value their wise mentoring.

During several months of research, I was assisted by Larry McQueen, Louis Morgan and the committed staff of the H.B. Dixon Pentecostal Research Center. They spared no efforts in locating the necessary documents I needed. I am also indebted to all those ministers who were so kind to share with me bits of information about their ministries.

During my stay in Cleveland I made many friends who influenced the pace of my research. I must also thank the Reverend David Williams who is the epitome of a perfect gentleman and scholar, Tack-Lin, Eriya, Tiffany, Wolfgang, Yves, Nelson, Nancy, Jung-hoon and many others. John T. Ramos, director of student services at the Church of God Theological Seminary, is to be commended for making my stay in Tennessee pleasant.

For many years now, my good friends Stephanie Sylvain, David P.A. Michel and Aly Jean-Louis have been a few of my best conversation partners. Also, many thanks to my brother, Asaph, and his lovely wife, Esther, for encouraging me; and to Maude and all the St. Forts for their collegiality.

Because of the timespan covered and the geographical extension of the black Church of God, it is not possible to identify all the heroes of the faith, much less to name them here.

Let us be reminded that at the judgment seat of Christ, every good deed will be acknowledged and the real motivations behind each of our actions will come to light

(2 Corinthians 5:10). It is only then that *all* the righteous will shine in full splendor (Matthew 13:43).

I must also thank Pathway Press for supporting this project, especially, Bill George, editor in chief, for his encouragement, and certainly the early reviewers for their valuable comments. In all, to God be the glory!

Introduction

When did blacks enter the Pentecostal Movement? What have they contributed to American Pentecostalism? What has been the major impact of American historical events upon black Pentecostals? And where do blacks in the Church of God fit into all of this? These questions must be addressed for the reader to appreciate the subject of this book.

Historians generally consider the Pentecostal Movement to have been birthed when Agnes Ozman, a student at the Topeka Bible School in Kansas, spoke Chinese on January 1, 1901, while praying for the Baptism of the Holy Spirit. Parham seems to have been the first American preacher to have clearly articulated the initial evidence doctrine, which links speaking in tongues to the Baptism of the Holy Spirit. Though he was a pioneer, Parham was not a major catalyst in the spreading of the movement across the United States and overseas. This honor was to be given to William J. Seymour, a son of former slaves. Seymour introduced many holiness preachers to the Pentecostal experience. Some of them in return led many southern blacks to seek the baptism of the Holy Spirit and affiliate with white Pentecostal churches. This was the beginning of the journey of blacks.

Telling the Story is the narration of the long and interesting pilgrimage of persons of African descent in the Church of God. Because of the time span covered and geographical extension of the blacks, it is not possible to tell the entire story of blacks in the Church of God.

Particular attention has been given to Florida, the pioneer state and the historic bulwark of the Black Church of God. Since the West Indians, along with their African-American brothers, have played important roles in the Church of God, a glimpse of their history will also be offered.

The black story needs to be told. Part 1 identifies the major events that occurred in the black church in North America and England. Part 2 surveys the biographical profiles of more than 20 African-American leaders, as well as the labors of 10 West Indian ministers.

I hope that through the following pages, we will gain appreciation for the rich heritage of black Pentecostals in the Church of God.

Part 1
Major Events in the Black Church

Chapter 1

The Early Beginnings 1884-1922

Today, there are estimated to be at least 7 million black Pentecostals in North America. They can be divided into four major groups. The first category includes the Original United Holy Church of America and the Church of God in Christ, both of which came out of non-Pentecostal black churches. Second, there are those bodies that split from black Pentecostal bodies: the Church of the Lord Jesus Christ of the Apostolic Faith, Bible Way Churches of Our Lord Jesus Christ Worldwide. These separated from the Pentecostal Assemblies of the World.

Another important part of the Pentecostal Movement is composed of denominations such as the Fire Baptized Holiness Church of the Americas and the Pentecostal Assemblies of the World, which exited from white Pentecostal denominations (in their case, the Fire Baptized Holiness Church and the initially white Pentecostal Assemblies of the World). There are many black Pentecostals in predominantly white churches, namely the Assemblies of God, the Pentecostal Holiness Church and the Church of God.

Telling the Story

In 1990, the number of blacks in these predominantly white denominations was estimated to be 40,000.

What have black Pentecostals contributed to American Pentecostalism and higher education? Scholars of religion still do not agree on the specific contributions of blacks. Because black and white churches in general ignored each other until the dissolution of the Pentecostal Fellowship of North America, there was not much cooperation between them for more than 80 years.

Nevertheless, Dr. Walter Hollenweger has ventured to propose that black Pentecostal music has impregnated much of white Pentecostalism. Much of the influence came through Garfield Haywood, a composer and leader of the Pentecostal Assemblies of the World, which had a large white following in the early days.

Black Pentecostals did not live in an ivory tower. They were impacted by contemporary events. At the end of the Civil War, blacks in white denominations such as the Southern Baptist Convention and the Methodist Episcopal Church South were made uneasy and chose to leave. Southern churches continued the segregationist practices, and the new Pentecostal churches adopted discriminatory practices. Below the Mason-Dixon line, blacks did not worship in the same churches as whites. Harsh racial conditions led millions of blacks to leave the deep South. It was those blacks who carried the message of Pentecost to urban cities such as New York and Baltimore. Those who chose to remain in the South migrated to urban areas where they could find work. Migrant workers moved to Florida and were instrumental in starting Church of God congregations there. The major event

The Early Beginnings 1884-1922

to impact black Pentecostals, especially those in white churches, was the civil rights movement—based mostly in the South. In the decades following the Civil Rights Act of 1964, blacks in predominantly white denominations started to agitate for full integration. In the '60s, mainline denominations passed resolutions on civil rights and integrated their Bible schools. The Church of God passed a resolution on human rights in 1964 and integrated in 1966.

Where do blacks in the Church of God fit in all this? The story of blacks in the Church of God is very important for several reasons. They are the strongest of all black groups operating within white Pentecostal denominations. There are more than 600 churches in the Church of God predominantly congregated by peoples of African descent. This black history is worth studying because it is directly linked to the Azusa Street revival.

The other distinguishing fact about blacks in this classic Pentecostal church is that they have contributed significantly to the denomination in the area of missions, church planting, and to a lesser degree, the field of education. A fair number of missionaries went to Africa to preach the gospel and to expand the ministry of the Church of God. A black educator was privileged to be the founding dean of the European Bible College in Germany. Later, he became the first president of Overstone Bible College, originally designed to upgrade the educational level of the black ministry in England. African-Americans have been a part of the Church of God for almost a century. Their journey with the church can be broken into five major time segments: 1909-1922, 1923-1930, 1931-1958, 1959-1966, 1967-present. The segment stretching from 1909 to 1966 can be called "the historic period" because this was when the blacks were under a dual government system. The new period from 1967 to the present is what I call the "modern era" of the black Church of God.

THE EARLY PERIOD

In 1886, a group of eight dispirited Baptists formed the Christian Union, a loose fellowship of believers who were deeply concerned about the loss of spirituality in their southern churches. Richard Spurling and his son, R.G. Spurling, (both Baptist ministers) were the leaders of this small group who met on August 19, 1886, in Monroe County, Tennessee. Their express purpose was to bring about a spiritual restoration to the church during those difficult times of the post-Civil War era.

As a charter member, R.G. Spurling was granted the full leadership of the Christian Union, and later united with another group in North Carolina led by W.F. Bryant, a Baptist deacon. In 1896, a revival swept through Cherokee County, North Carolina, that introduced the practices of speaking in tongues and divine healing to more than 100 people. Influenced by the Fire Baptized Holiness Church, these "new" Pentecostals became affected by all kinds of excesses, which almost wrecked the continued growth of the Christian Union. Because the Union was experiencing a significant loss in membership, Spurling and Bryant thought it necessary to formally organize their little band into a church. This is why on May 15, 1902, about 20 people convened to set in order the "Holiness Church at Camp Creek" with R. G. Spurling as pastor.

The Early Beginnings 1884-1922

The next most significant event in this new holiness church occurred about a year later. A.J. Tomlinson, a former Quaker, accepted the right hand of fellowship after claiming a supernatural revelation from God to do so. No one then had any hints that in the next 20 years, the life of this mountain church would be greatly dependent upon the genius of their new pastor.

In December 1904, Tomlinson moved to Cleveland, Tennessee, and by 1905 there were reports of four new congregations. This move to Cleveland was important because it permitted the church to maintain easy communication with the world beyond Appalachia, due to the proximity of the railroad service.

In 1907 G.B. Cashwell went to Los Angeles and visited the mission at Azusa Street, seeking the Baptism of the Holy Spirit. After being prayed for by a young black, he received the full blessing, and immediately sought to win his fellow southerners to the Pentecostal faith. Cashwell captured the attention of A.J. Tomlinson, then moderator of the Church of God, who invited him to preach at the Third General Assembly of the Church of God in 1908. Cashwell preached the Sunday morning following the General Assembly. During the message, Tomlinson received the Baptism of the Holy Spirit for the first time and claimed to have spoken in 10 different languages. Through Cashwell, Tomlinson links the blacks in the Church of God to William Seymour, the leader of the Azusa Street revival.

By 1909 Cleveland was a small community with a population approaching 1,000. A careful reading of the *Minutes* of that year indicates that the membership of the Church of God was at least 300 by the time of the Fourth General Assembly early in the year. The number of churches remained small—only about eight churches.

The year 1909 was very important in the history of the Church of God. It was then that Tomlinson was made general moderator and given the authority to issue credentials to prospective ministers. This year also bears significance in black history, because it was in 1909 that blacks began to enter the fellowship. In that year a Bahamian couple, Edmond and Rebecca Barr, received the Baptism of the of the Holy Spirit and consequently entered the Church of God. With the Barrs, the black journey began in the church.

FLORIDA: THE PIONEER STATE, 1909-1922

In 1909 Edmond Barr and his wife, Rebecca, joined the Church of God. Barr was soon licensed and started to preach the gospel in the surrounding communities. He ministered to a young man named Sampson Ellis Everett, whom he led to the Pentecostal experience. Everett, returned to his hometown of Jacksonville, Florida, and won his family to the message of Pentecost. His family later became the nucleus of the famous Jacksonville Church of God—the first African-American congregation in the Church of God. Florida was the birthplace of the black work and eventually served as the center of evangelism for what was later called the Church of God Colored Work.

Due to the evangelistic fervor of these new Pentecostals, the fire of Pentecost spread to Coconut Grove and Webster, Florida—the other earliest black

The Early Beginnings 1884-1922

congregations to be recorded in the official minutes. Between 1909 and 1915, seven black congregations were established, and the leadership began to consider appointing a black leader to supervise the blacks in Florida. At the General Assembly of 1915, Barr was appointed the first black state overseer. The segregated structure was dissolved in 1917 when Barr was replaced by Sam C. Perry, a white minister, who assumed the leadership of both white and black congregations in Florida.

Chapter 2

Expanded Autonomy 1923-1966

In 1922 a delegation from Florida went to the General Assembly and made a request to Overseer Tomlinson that a black be appointed to oversee the African-American congregations. After much hesitation, the Committee on Better Government recommended that Thomas Richardson, a minister from Miami who was doing evangelistic work in North Carolina, be the next national overseer. He did not remain long. When Tomlinson was dismissed in 1923, he left with him.

David LaFleur, a former deacon, replaced Richardson and served for the next six years while also working as a local pastor. LaFleur was a visionary. He made major decisions that were to have great impact upon the future of black churches. One of his commendable actions was to call an assembly of the black churches in 1925.

Annual Assemblies. At the General Assembly of 1926, the denomination ratified the previous decision of LaFleur to hold annual assemblies. These assemblies played a significant role in the lives of the black people. Not only did they allow the leaders to deal with business and governmental issues, but they also allowed the membership as a whole to enjoy their own fellowship without restraint. Due to the mores of the South, blacks attending the General Assembly had to sit in a reserved section, apart from whites. The Church of God black congregations developed a sense of belonging and self-affirmation from these ethnic assemblies.

Missionary Thrust. During LaFleur's leadership, an evangelistic thrust was felt and acted upon—funds were set aside for foreign and home missions. There was some interest in reaching out to the Bahamas. On the domestic soil, three missionaries were assigned to plant churches in the North. LaFleur's successors maintained his evangelistic program, even enlarged it. To further allow their overseer to commit himself to his work, the Elders Council voted to relieve him of his pastoral duties.

Sunday School and Youth Work. Sunday school had a late start among the blacks. In 1923 G. Sapp, an aggressive minister, set up the first Sunday school in Jupiter, Florida. Sapp, looking after the welfare of black youths, introduced the Young People's Endeavor program (then called Young People's Missionary Band) to the Sanford Church of God. Three years later Uriah P. Bronson, a public school principal, agreed to be the state Sunday school superintendent. Bronson, who was educated and progressive thinker, was also responsible for the organization of the youth work. In 1928, Bronson was made chairman of the state youth ministry.

Social and Educational Ventures. Since the 18th century, the black church has been known to be the most important African-American institution. The role of the church increased with the abolition of slavery and the failure of Reconstruction. In order to improve their lot, American blacks developed a tradition of self-help. Out of this background emerged the social and educational initiatives of black Pentecostals. Blacks in the Church of God were no different from their peers. Also, the corporate church provided stimuli for social and educational endeavors among the blacks, already having sponsored a Bible school and orphanage and refurbished an auditorium by 1920. As early as 1927, plans were discussed and later ratified for the organization of an orphanage and school, a burial auxiliary, a fund for disabled ministers, and the construction of an auditorium to hold the growing colored assemblies.

Consolidated Autonomy and National Organization, 1930-1957

In 1928, LaFleur resigned and was replaced by J.H. Curry, a native of the Bahamas. Curry led the church to great expansion in major areas. Under him, the black work would finally have a real national structure. Up to the time of LaFleur, the state overseer of Florida was unofficially recognized as the national leader for all blacks. The problem with this arrangement is that there were no other state overseers or state structures, and the northern churches were scattered. To resolve the loose affiliation of the northern congregations, Curry requested from General Overseer Latimer that they be consolidated with the Florida-based southern churches. He wanted the Florida overseer to be the overseer of the black constituents in the North instead of the white state overseers. Latimer agreed and consenting northern pastors came under the leadership of the colored overseer at the General Assembly of 1930. Another major decision was

Telling the Story

reached in 1932 when both a general YPE president, a general Sunday school superintendent and other black state overseers were appointed. It was the first time that the term *general* (meaning "national") was linked to the appointments. The black church had come of age.

A significant accomplishment of Curry was the partial completion of a building program. Land was bought for $1,600 at Eustis in 1927, and the Church of God Industrial School and Orphanage was dedicated in 1934. In 1936 the Jacksonville Auditorium, which was also a sanctuary, was inaugurated. It was built primarily through the efforts of the ladies auxiliary groups. At the time of its first dedication, the value of this auditorium was $25,000. With these two buildings, the blacks created something that they could be proud of — something they did not receive from outsiders, but was the work of their hands. The builder and pastor of the auditorium was a black minister, C.F. Bright.

The last thing to be said about Curry's administration is his emphasis on Bible training. By 1931, one Bible school was being operated in the Sunshine State. In 1932, the Bishops' Council recommended that a theological seminary be initiated.

At the end of Curry's overseership, the major foundation of the black Church of God was laid. In 1938, when Norbert Marcelle took the helm, he could only build on the foundations. Though Marcelle united the Sunday school and the YPE, his major emphasis was to eliminate the debt incurred for the auditorium. He finally succeeded in paying the balance of $1,541.74 in 1942. During his tenure (1938-1946), these three amendments and decisions were made by the general church:

Expanded Autonomy 1923-1966

- That the colored ordained ministers and male licensed ministers be privileged to express to the General Executive Committee their desire for their overseer and the final decision of appointment be vested in the General Executive Committee.

- That the overseer of the colored work be appointed by the General Executive Committee at the Assembly of the colored people.

- That the colored people be granted the privilege of opening a Bible school.[1]

After Marcelle, one of the main concerns of the black overseers continued to be the reduction of debt in the ministry. Willie Ford (1946-1950; 1954-1958), a seasoned administrator who succeeded Marcelle, cleared the debt on the orphanage and school and kept these institutions working through a reduction of personnel and an increase in tuition fees. The highlight of Bishop Wallace's term (1950-1954) was the completion of the Jacksonville Auditorium and the formalization of the Ladies Ministry Auxiliary. In 1952, Mrs. Shirley Wallace was made the first president of the Black Ladies Willing Worker Band. Black women in the church had made history. In 1954, the National Missions Department was organized to maintain the evangelistic program of the black work.

A Period of Relative Autonomy, 1958-1966

The '50s rolled in with a growing concern of the general church to expand the black work, aggravated by deteriorating race relations. In 1951, the Church of God

Telling the Story

considered removing the black national overseer, but did not proceed with this idea at the time. By the second half of the century, blacks started to complain about subjugation in the church. This tense period has been labeled the "African-American Dilemma" by Charles Conn.

> The comparative lack of growth among the blacks was a nagging concern to the white leadership of the church. The Executive Committee and Supreme Council gave occasional consideration to ways of increasing black growth and involvement in general church outreach. Ironically, that concern led to miscalculations and tensions that were painful to both blacks and whites. In the setting of that period, answers were difficult to find, or they were typically superficial. In many ways the Church of God reflected the national frustration and inertia of the times.[2]

A critical year in the history of the black Church of God was 1958. For the first time a non-black national overseer was appointed. For 35 years, black leaders had been given almost free rein to lead their constituency. This change in leadership contested black confidence in self-rule. Charles Conn, now official historian of the Church of God, but who was then editor in chief of the *Evangel*, the denominational magazine, has thus captured the mood of the black leaders at the time.

> There was no question of their loyalty to the Church of God, for many of them had been a part of the church longer than most white members. They simply wanted African-American leadership of their endeavors, an understandable desire.[3]

Expanded Autonomy 1923-1966

J.T. Roberts, the new overseer, was not unknown to the blacks. He had pastored in Florida, and had served as state overseer of Alabama and Florida. Aware of the mixed feelings toward him, Roberts presented an ambitious program in his acceptance speech.

> I am not put here to be lord over you but we are going to work together. I shall do all that I can to promote the growth of the work among the youth of the church. It is up to us to get the youth what they need. We can have a college. We are on a well-rounded program in the church, Sunday School and everything.[4]

At this same colored assembly, a young black woman, Bernice Douse, was appointed national Sunday school and youth director for the colored work. She was previously the assistant to E.D. Cobbs, head of the department for 10 years and also a peerless preacher.

Roberts will go down in history, perhaps as a controversial figure, but nevertheless as a progressive leader. An article in the *Evangel* reported that he was quite convincing when dealing with bank examiners about building loans for his constituency. As a result, over 100 church buildings were built during his overseership. To improve ministerial training, Roberts invited Lee College teachers to Florida to conduct four-week training seminars in Jacksonville and Philadelphia in 1959 and 1960. More than 180 students enrolled in the Jacksonville Bible Institutes, and 104 participants attended the seminar in Philadelphia, Pennsylvania. In 1960, it was deemed advisable to appoint a national youth board to maintain equality with the General Assembly. The first members

Telling the Story

of this board were C.F. Bright Jr., Alice Matthews, Shirley Wallace, T.L. Hayes, and K.L. Woodside. At the 1960 Colored Assembly, a recommendation was made to establish a national Bible college for black people.

In 1965, Roberts resigned. In his farewell address, he summarized his accomplishments as follows:

> Our total membership increased from 2,931 to 7,360. From 102 churches in 19 states we have grown to a national size of 214 churches in 24 states. From no full-time employees we now have two full-time employees, the National Sunday School and Youth Director and the Secretary to the Overseer, whose salaries are comparable to those of comparable workers in the secular world.[5]

To replace J.T. Roberts, another non-black overseer, David Lemons, was appointed. According to the general overseer, the number of votes received by black candidates was too low to warrant the selection of a black leader. The new overseer did not have time to do much, because in 1966, the denomination voted for integration during a time of fierce civil rights activities in the United States. A staff writer for the *Evangel* made the following comment in 1972.

> In the meantime, the social climate of the country was changing in regard to civil rights, and the church was changing with it. In 1964, the Church of God ordained ministers passed a resolution on human rights which stated the church's view on racial segregation. It urged that no "American be deprived of his right to worship, vote, rest, eat, sleep, be educated, live, and work on the same basis as other citizens."[6]

Expanded Autonomy 1923-1966

Roberts, a member of the Council of Twelve, presented a resolution to the church about integration. He was instrumental in leading the church to adopt a fresh commitment and ending segregation.

The church integrated in 1966, and for the first time, African-Americans were given the opportunity to enter Lee University. The national black judicatory was dissolved, and the position of overseer of the colored work was eliminated. Black state overseers were made district overseers, and a black liaison office was established at the Church of God International Offices. The first and only person to fill this position was the Reverend H.G. Poitier.

The period 1909-1966 was not an easy one for blacks in the Church of God. Though many chose to remain in the church in spite of the problems encountered, others were more radical and chose to leave. In 1922 there was a major exodus of black ministers. Between 1939 and 1941, 20 churches were disbanded and a loss of 667 members was reported.

Chapter 3

The Historic Black Church of God

In 1909, the first African-American congregation in the Church of God was founded in Jacksonville, Florida. Today African-Americans worship in more than 300 congregations in the United States.

We have just surveyed the history of the black church. It will be interesting to take a look at the factors that have contributed to making what it is today.

1909-1958

Blacks have a long history in the Church of God. Hispanics, as a minority group, can also trace their history to the early decades of this century within this denomination. Many elements coalesced from the very beginning to challenge the African-American churches to expand their constituency. The most influential factors included the following: the personality and legacy of A. J. Tomlinson, immigration, sacrificial ministry, progressive leadership and the influential role of women.

Ambrose J. Tomlinson and the Beginnings of the Black Work. Reverend Tomlinson licensed Edmond Barr after Barr received the Baptism of the Spirit. After returning from a preaching tour in the Bahamas, Barr was ordained and in 1915, arose to a position of leadership over the black churches in Florida. He was dismissed in 1917. By 1922 blacks were changing to other denominations. To curtail this exodus, Tomlinson finally consented, upon recommendation of the black clergymen, to provide an autonomous structure for the blacks instead of keeping them under the white leaders. Three years before, he broke tradition by calling on blacks to participate in the services at the General Assembly. Prior to 1919, blacks had only been "spectators" at the General Assembly and were not asked to be a part of the program. Tomlinson was an innovator and perhaps unique in contemporary American Pentecostalism with his bold moves to involve blacks in the corporate governmental structure of the church. He and the Council of Twelve also appointed four black men to the Council of Seventy. They were W. Eneas, W. Franks, Thomas B. Smith and Thomas J. Richardson. Following in the footsteps of Reverend Tomlinson, F.J. Lee and S.W. Latimer allowed blacks to hold their own assemblies and elect their own overseers. They appointed David LaFleur and John Curry to the Council of Seventy and the Council of Twelve, respectively.

Immigration

The Barrs were the first blacks to join the Church of God. They went on to evangelize other blacks in the Bahamas. Many British West Indians were already living in the southern states. By late 19th century, about 1,000

The Historic Black Church of God

West Indians had entered the United States. From 1900 to 1930, 80,000 to 90,000 immigrants settled in Florida, New York and Massachusetts. Among them were 3,000 Bahamians who worked on farms in Florida and in the construction business in South Carolina. These West Indians must have formed good targets for Pentecostal soulwinners. E.L. Simmons, the first historian of the Church of God, reports that the first black (West Indian) Church of God in Miami was composed mostly of immigrants from the Bahamas. Most likely, it was Barr who first preached to his fellow natives. Following him, other immigrants evangelized and planted at least three congregations in Florida.

The Bahamians could easily mingle with native blacks because they spoke the same language. Because of other cultural affinities, they intermarried with African-Americans and became leaders in the black church. Edmond Barr, J.H. Curry and H.G. Poitier were among the most prominent leaders who were born overseas. Barr was state overseer and Curry the second national overseer of the Colored Work.

The Influential Role of Women. Much can be said about the influential role of women in African-American culture. During the colonial period, women played a significant role in the black society and the black church. Though black women were first ordained only by the African Methodists, they were nonetheless responsible in various ways for the progress of the black church throughout its existence, probably because of the high female membership of its congregations. No history of the black Church of God would be complete without mentioning the accomplishments of these daughters of Zion.

Telling the Story

Women served in the black churches primarily as evangelists, church planters and administrators. Janet Spencer in *Black Women in the Church* asserts that they roamed the whole United States preaching revivals. In the state of Florida, more than 15 women preachers worked during this historic period. A greater number of these women operated in the northern regions, at least 21. Altogether, about 36 women evangelists reaped the harvest of souls in black communities during the history of the black Church of God.

Though women could not pastor, many were in charge of local congregations. What stood out is not the fact that they preached revivals, but rather that they also distinguished themselves as church planters. More than 60 congregations were founded by women during the historic period of the black Church of God. The number of congregations founded by any particular woman varies from 1 to 21.

- Arlene Dean is credited with pioneering over 20 churches in Alabama during her preaching tours.
- Janice Denson and her husband also pioneered probably 12 churches.
- Emily and Flora Miller, from the Bahamas, planted numerous churches in the Florida area.

Women also performed administrative duties. Many of the clerks in the black congregations were women. Some women were more conspicuous in terms of leadership. They were in charge of the orphanage and industrial school. Some became president of the National Missions Committee.

The Historic Black Church of God

When the Orphanage was dedicated in 1934, Jessie L. Hayward was named general president. In the same capacity, Ethel Coleman served two years, Susie Bronson two years, Melissa Marcelle six years and Maggie Brantley two years. For five years Brantley headed the Committee for the Completion of the Jacksonville Auditorium.

Progressive Leadership. Many of the early black leaders came out of the African Methodist Episcopal Church, the Christian Methodist Episcopal Church and various types of Baptist confessions operating in the South. They brought their previous experience with them to the Church of God. Peter C. Hickson worked with youth and served as a Baptist deacon before joining the Church of God. Uriah P. Bronson was a public school principal who promoted Sunday school extensively among his people. Wallace and Marcelle opened local Bible schools in their districts. Some, like W. Eneas and Eugene Cobbs, attended the Bible Training School in order to improve their ministry. Curry, as overseer, endorsed the idea of constructing the Jacksonville Auditorium, which was destined to be the next arena for the annual black assemblies. The black work was blessed with gifted people to promote the Church of God.

Sacrificial Ministry. Ministry in the early 20th century was no sinecure for southern black circuit riders. They had to reckon with Jim Crow. Charles Conn labels their nightmare "The Double Difficulty."

> Whatever was hard on white preachers, male or female was manifold worse for African-Americans. Before, during, and long after the Depression, travel and labor

for them was a logistical nightmare. Any restaurant where they might find food was always for whites only. Unless they learned that somewhere ahead, in some across-the-tracks section of some out-of-the-way town, there was a place where they might secure food, they had to do without. Lacking restaurants where they were welcome, the black Church of God brethren ate whatever they bought at a grocery store and carried in a sack. They ate by the side of the road and found rest facilities wherever they could. Water fountains were almost designated for "whites only," and the possibility of finding toilet facilities available to them was virtually out of question. Being a black Pentecostal preacher during the Depression (or any other time) presented difficulties not even imagined by most of society.[1]

Many pastors served several congregations at the same time. It is reported that Peter Hickson walked five miles after working 10 hours to reach his preaching appointment. It was this kind of unselfish attitude that allowed the church to grow.

The Church of God and Black Evangelism Since 1958

Institutional concerns. Since integration, there has been a major concern from the general church to engage in black evangelism. In 1968 W.C. Menendez, a former state overseer of New Jersey, was appointed as missionary evangelist to work in black cities. A Bible institute program was inaugurated in Florida in 1971 to provide training to both black clergy and laity for evangelistic work. In 1972 Wallace Sibley, then state youth director in Florida, vented his concern for evangelism among his people.

The Historic Black Church of God

> The blacks in the United States are a veritable mission field on the church's door step. America's black population exceeds 24 million. Many are unchurched and in need of the gospel. I believe that the entire Church of God family would benefit, if more black ministers could be trained in evangelism and supported in a concentrated outreach to the black community.[2]

Two years later, Alphonso Slaughter became the first black national evangelist.

An appreciation for this appointment can best be read from J.D. Nichols, who was then responsible for home evangelism.

> I think a historic event for the Church of God was the appointment of the first national black evangelist. In our many interviews, I have detected a genuine burden and real concerns for souls. I feel that the black community will feel the effect of this man and his concern.[3]

Without belittling these previous efforts, the Reverend Dr. T.L. Lowery, a prominent healing evangelist, was the first to encourage the corporate church in a vigorous effort of black outreach. Dr. Lowery, assistant general overseer, served for six years (1976-1982) as the representative of black affairs and supervised the black church during its evangelistic thrust. He worked vigorously to win the black harvest.

> It is my dream that those black people, who frequently seek liberty through avenues that too often lead only to further bondage, will find, through the efforts of black Church of God ministers and

Telling the Story

laymen, the only real freedom possible—that which is in Christ.[4]

To address this evangelistic thrust, Dr. Lowery initiated the following measures.

- He conducted a national survey of black problems and appointed a Committee on Ethnic Affairs. Wallace Sibley was a part of this committee.

- He sponsored outreach seminars in several cities. The most important of these was the one that met in Cleveland in March 1978, when both white and black leaders engaged in serious dialogue on the issue of outreach. The outcome of this seminar was the creation of a regional office for black evangelism at the General Assembly. Wallace Sibley was its first leader and because of his hard work, the office was made a national agency in 1983.

- In 1986, Jimmy Campbell, state council member from Georgia, was appointed to the National Evangelism and Home Missions Board, where he served until 1994. He was the first black to serve on such a board.

Chapter 4

Evangelism in the Black Church

For many years, Florida remained the strongest focus of black outreach. It was at the Colored Assembly of 1928 that, for the first time, missionary evangelists were dispatched to southern fields. At the 1929 Colored Assembly, several missionaries were again sent to the South: G. Sapp, Alabama; C.F. Bright, Georgia; Ernest Ford, Arkansas; W.M. Stewart, Mississippi; and Ed Johnson, Kentucky.

The Black Belt

Though these early efforts were admirable, it was not until J.T. Roberts took the leadership of the black churches that a serious effort would be made to reap the harvest in the Black Belt. During his administration (1958-1965), a considerable number of female state evangelists were deployed to many unreached areas. Reverend C.C. Daniels, who was made overseer of Arkansas and Mississippi during Roberts' tenure, claims that it was under Roberts administration that the black work experienced a major increase.

According to Bishop Asbury Sellers, during the civil rights movement the black church was standing firm on the Word of God, evangelizing and establishing churches. It appears, however, that this growth (especially in the Deep South) subsided after integration. Because of uneasy race relations, blacks were reluctant to associate with white churches and other black Pentecostal denominations such as the Church of God in Christ and the Fire Baptized Holiness Church of the Americas.

Black Outreach

The Church of God experienced extreme difficulties in consolidating its gains and opening new missions during this time. Stories have emerged about affiliated congregations that left the Church of God in order to join other black groups in the '60s. In 1971 black people started to alert the leadership about the need to appoint black evangelists. In 1974 Reverend Alphonso Slaughter talked to J.D. Nichols, director of evangelism and home missions, about letting a black man work with a state evangelism director so the blacks would identify with the state leadership.

Such concerns received greater attention after a report released by Winston Elliott (a church-growth expert then teaching at Lee University), which revealed that 40 percent of the black growth in membership between 1966 and 1977 took place in Florida. Like Mississippi, Florida had remained a black judicatory even after integration. The logical interpretation of Elliott's report was unescapable: black preachers were more successful at reaching their own, and African-Americans were more likely to make it to the altar when the revivalist was black — especially in the South. At a seminar on black outreach that convened in March 1978, the issue of black outreach was forcefully articulated by those black ministers who attended. It was argued that lack of black visibility and lack of emphasis on black achievements in church publications was hindering the appeal of the Church of God to reach black prospects. Presentations were made at this seminar by James Campbell, Cyril Pratt, Willie Vaughn, Wallace Sibley, C.C. Pratt and W.C. Menendez.

Expansion in the Southern States

At the General Assembly the same year, Wallace Sibley was placed in charge of black outreach in the following southern states: Mississippi, Alabama, North and South Carolina, North and South Georgia and Tennessee. Let us review the expansion of the work in the southern states.

Mississippi. Without doubt, Sibley laid the groundwork for the current expansion of the black work. His labors were productive in the organization of 55 new congregations during a four-year period (1978-1982). His methods combined familiarizing blacks to the church, promoting the hiring of black evangelists and creating channels for ethnic fellowship. In March 1979, a seminar on black enrichment was organized in St. Mary's, Georgia. According to the *South Georgia Accent*, "The intent of the seminar was to introduce to the Church of God some of our officials, to acquaint them to the church, and to help them bring their local church and district to state, and general programs."[1] The regional director led a workshop that was attended by 358 people. Sibley was familiar with the terrain, having pastored there and served as South Georgia's liaison for black affairs. In North Georgia, one black church was planted by Joe Pierce in 1979.

Telling the Story

Sibley was sensitive to the need for black deployment in evangelism. "Blacks must evangelize blacks. We have the message and the power. With sufficient funds, we could win America for God."[2] Faithful to himself, Sibley sought out black evangelists for endorsement. In the fall of 1978, David Greenlee, a pastor in Pennsylvania, was made full-time field evangelist in Mississippi. In June 1979, Greenlee was again promoted to ethnic director. In a less than a year, he was able to organize two churches (Macedonia in Indianola and Maranatha in Moss Point) and four missions (Vicksburg, Bruce, Jackson and Tunica).

In August 1979, Northeast Mississippi inaugurated the first meeting of the Mississippi Black Fellowship Conference, which was attended by more than 300 delegates. This conference was meant to accomplish in the South what the Northeast Regional Fellowship did in other regions of the country — provide a forum for ethnic fellowship in the Church. This meeting was so blessed, on the last day 14 new members and two ministers were received into the Church of God. These ministers were selected to assume the pastorates of new churches, adding to those that had already been planted by C.C. Daniels, a longtime black pastor and a former overseer of Arkansas and Mississippi.

Alabama. In 1958, J.T. Roberts assigned a group of evangelists, mostly women, to Alabama (Arlene Dean, A.J. Bell, S.E. Babbs, Ella O. Poole and Verba Mae Mayo). Their state overseer was Preston Gardner. These women fanned out to share the good news, like Mary Magdalene did 2,000 years ago. Alabama has a long history of women trailblazers. In 1926, Sister Mary Ash preached a revival in Flat Top, and the first black

Evangelism in the Black Church

Church of God was organized there in the same year. Other female pioneers in Alabama opened churches in Lapine, Talledega and Birmingham. The most vigorous evangelist in the state in those early years was Arlene Dean, who is believed to have planted no less than 21 churches in Alabama alone!

After integration, W.C. Menendez, a metro evangelist, revitalized black outreach in Alabama and planted a mission church in Pritchard in 1969. During the period 1970-1972, two churches and two missions were established in Alabama. In 1976-77, the Bridge Avenue Church of God, a black congregation, was organized in Tuscaloosa. In the '80s, Charles Marcelle, the first black youth director of New York Metro, worked with Bill Sheeks, state overseer of Alabama, and was instrumental in organizing these six black congregations: North Birmingham, Word Revival, Gadsden Central, Troy, North Birmingham, Philadelphia and West End.

North and South Carolina. When J.T. Roberts took over in 1958, Julius Geiger and Grover Reed were assigned as overseers to North and South Carolina, respectively. Evangelists assigned to these two states were: Ruby Carson, Bertha Cobbs, Lelia Anthony, Marion Geiger, Dollie Stanley and Elizabeth Geiger. Prior to them, the first black preacher assigned to preach in North Carolina was C.F. Bright in 1931.

Julius Geiger, district overseer of the Palimco district, was one of those who maintained a loyal commitment to increasing the work of the Lord in the Carolinas. He has preached for more than 40 years and extended the kingdom of God with the planting of four black churches.

Telling the Story

Gertrude Sellers was another pioneer in the Carolinas. As a an evangelist, she preached quite a few revivals and organized several congregations, among them the United Church of God and the Mount Hermon Church of God. Two of her sons, Bishops Asbury and Nathan Sellers, followed her in the ministry. They, in turn, inherited her church planting abilities.

Another hard worker was Bishop Lee Wade Mintz who pastored 44 years in Orangeburg, South Carolina. He is noted for his wise guidance of the southern black churches during the tumultuous era of the civil rights movement.

In North Carolina, Curtis Grey did magnificent work. Coming from Liberia, he was appointed as the first director of black affairs for North Carolina in 1981. Prior to his appointment, the black work in North Carolina was in disarray and many congregations were inactive. Grey worked there for more than three years and accumulated 110,000 miles in ministerial travels, organizing 17 churches. About 30 ministers became licensed, and a black convention was instituted to rally the sheep under the umbrella of the Church of God.

For the last 18 years, Nathan Sellers, black coordinator of North Carolina, has consolidated and expanded the work under his dynamic leadership. Bishop Sellers established the first black Church of God in Fayetteville, East Carolina. His commitment to evangelism allowed him to later plant six more congregations out of his local church.

Georgia and Tennessee. The first missionary evangelist ever to be appointed to Georgia was C.F. Bright. In 1928, a decision was reached — missionaries must be sent to the southern states. Bright was among the missionaries com-

Evangelism in the Black Church

missioned to evangelism work in 1929. In 1931, John Russ was appointed missionary to Georgia, and Bright was made overseer of Georgia and North Carolina. It was not too long before Georgia was blossoming with new black congregations. Through the work of T.W. Wimberly, a church was established in St. Mary's in 1932. In its early days, the members worshiped in the home of Flossie Williams and her husband. Alice Wheeler, a member of the community, attended this church, which later took her name. For many years, St. Mary's was a mother church, the largest in Georgia.

As the years went by, congregations were established at Augusta, Brunswick, Cedar Park, Cedartown, Eastman, Hawkinsville, Kingsland, Lavonia, Pineview, Rochelle and Savannah.

J.T. Roberts continued the evangelistic thrust that was started by Bright by appointing Raymond Campbell, Mary Etta Stocks and Mattie Lee Showers as state evangelists in 1958. Roberts was concerned about the expansion of the black work in Georgia. In 1963, 17 evangelists were appointed to do outreach work in that state. In that same year, only Florida deployed a greater number of evangelists.

In the early '70s, two churches were planted at Columbus and Eastman. In 1976-77, two churches and one mission were established. On March 21, 1977, the Hazelhurst Church of God was set in order with nine members and Raymond Campbell as pastor. On July 19, 1977, Reverend Williams and nine members formed the Bainbridge Church of God. In Jessup, Pastor Jerome Jackson maintained a mission with about 20 people.

Telling the Story

Frankie McDonald, state liaison for black affairs in Georgia, contributed in promoting church planting. Today there are 18 black congregations in south Georgia, all the result of sacrificial work of the pioneers.

The black work in Tennessee had an early start. In 1913, the first black church was organized in Betsytown with Margaret Collier as clerk. This church did not last long. Nevertheless, there may have been a few blacks in other towns who affiliated with the Church of God. Only P.G. Talley of Hamble, Tennessee, was listed as an ordained minister in the 1914 *General Assembly Minutes*.

Today, the oldest black church in Tennessee is the Inman Street Church of God, organized in the '40s. In the second half of this century, a main catalyst for church planting in Tennessee was Leola McLain. At a very young age, she received a call to the ministry and was sent to pastor the Rockford Church of God in Pikeville around 1959. Trusting God, she committed herself to the pastorate and was able to refurbish the old sanctuary and dedicate a new one—the Wheeler Addition Church of God. Through her evangelistic orientation, Reverend McLain planted two other churches in Johnson City and Dayton. In 1941, Bishop C.L. Drummond managed to pioneer a new church in Knoxville while living in Kentucky. Later, he and his family moved there in order to more effectively assume this pastorate. In 1963, there were seven black churches in Tennessee organized into four districts with W.H. Eddington, V.S. Beckford and C.L. Drummond as overseers.

Evangelism in the Northern States

The first black northerner to be credentialed in the

Evangelism in the Black Church

Church of God was Daniel Davis, an ordained preacher from Philadelphia, Pennsylvania. His name appears in the *Minutes of the 13th General Assembly*. Nevertheless, it was only in 1924 that Garfield Byrd would organize the first Church of God in Pittsburgh, Pennsylvania—the Northside congregation. This was the first black church planted in the North. At the Fifth Black Annual Assembly, Garfield Byrd and J.W. Hamilton were commissioned as missionaries to the North. At this same assembly, Byrd was ordained as a bishop, the highest ministerial rank in the church. The following year, Hamilton was sent as missionary to New Jersey. In 1931, Byrd and Hamilton became the overseers of Pennsylvania and New Jersey, respectively. Black northerners were liberal and did not follow those blacks below the Mason-Dixon line. They did not acquiesce to segregation as a means for appeasement and an avenue to progress. When F.J. Lee granted southern congregations the right to organize an annual assembly, northern blacks complained, requested and secured from Lee the right to remain part of the white General Assembly at their discretion. For a while, the black judicatory that was operating out of Florida was only loosely associated with the black churches in the North. This schism was diffused when Bishop Curry pressured the church at large to consolidate the entire black work in 1930. By 1938, they were at least five congregations in Pennsylvania and New Jersey.

Bishop Marcelle, overseer of New York and New Jersey, worked with Florine Hurt to plant a church in Freehold, New Jersey, in 1946. In the '40s and '50s, Marcelle planted several congregations in the Brooklyn section of New York at Third Avenue, Gates Avenue and Sackman Avenue. In Rochester, New York, evangelist Mary Dixon preached a revival where eight souls were saved. She organized these new converts into a church in the mid-'50s and became their pastor. In 1963 Mildred and Julian Cox, who attended the congregation pastored by Mary Dixon, moved to another part of town and planted the Goodman Street Church of God. The work in New York expanded and 15 churches were divided in three districts by 1963. For this same year, New Jersey reported nine churches and Pennsylvania 13 congregations.

In 1958, only in Pennsylvania, New Jersey and New York was the black Church of God represented in the North. When Roberts left in 1965, black congregations were listed in Rhode Island, Connecticut and Massachusetts. District overseers were: Edgar McNeil in Massachusetts; Alphonso and W.C. Menendez in New Jersey; H.L. Blackwell, Cyril Pratt, Elijah Holmes; N.S. Marcelle, E.D. Cobbs, Horace Johnson, John Davis, Clarence Denson in Pennsylvania. In the '60s, Earl Bright, who pastored in Fayetteville, North Carolina, moved to Providence, Rhode Island, where he was able to establish the Beacon Avenue Church of God.

Other Regions

In the District of Columbia, Pastors Asbury Sellers and Enus Gordon did an appreciable labor through metro evangelism. Sellers pioneered eight congregations in the Washington/Baltimore area. In 1966, Pastor Sellers resigned his pastorate in North Carolina to plant the Capitol Church of God. By 1971, this church had

Evangelism in the Black Church

about 125 members. After graduating from Lee University in 1977, Enus and Jane Gordon moved to Washington D.C., and gathered a few people in their dining room. By 1977, their membership was over 100.

The Church of God was slow to reap the black harvest in the Southwest. The work in Texas was initiated under Roberts. In 1961-1963, Louis Banks, from Houston, Texas, joined the Church of God with his congregation. In 1965, Horace Spragg became the overseer (1965-1972) of the black work in Texas. By 1970 the church had reached the blacks in California, and two churches were reported to be in existence in Los Angeles. Between 1970-1972, two other congregations were organized in that city: Florence Avenue and Central Street. In 1976, Horace Marshall was assigned to Los Angeles as metro evangelist.

In the Northwest Willie Vaughn, who joined the Church of God in the mid-'60s, became the ethnic director for Oregon and Washington in 1974 and planted more than 10 new churches in that region.

In the Midwest, Naomi Lawler and her husband pioneered four congregations in Indiana (Gary, Indianapolis) and Illinois (Chicago and Evanston). The Gary Church of God came out of prayer services started in her house in 1948. During 1976-77, three black churches were organized in Chicago and Champaign, Illinois. From 1978 to 1982 Billy Rayburn, overseer of Chicago Metro, worked with Charles Sanders, a black preacher, to consolidate the black ministries in this metropolis.

When Sibley's tenure ended in 1982, Dr. C.C. Pratt became regional evangelism director of black ministries and actively promoted the interest of the black work at

Telling the Story

the international level. He was followed by Dr. Joseph E. Jackson, who served until 1998. The current director, Dr. Asbury Sellers, is a former national evangelist and greatly in demand, because of his dynamic preaching. As national evangelist, he was replaced in 1994 by William Lee, Jr., who was a graduate of Lee University. Lee has received high marks for his skillful delivery, earning the reputation of a cross-cultural preacher. He preached at the last General Assembly and is highly sought after as a guest speaker, nationally and internationally.

At the 1998 General Assembly the following people were appointed to the Board of Directors of Black Ministries: Wallace Sibley, chairperson; Quan Miller and Selwyn Arnold, advisors; Robert E. Brookins, Wardell Avant Jr., Thomas Chenault, Joscelyn William and Jimmy Campbell.

Chapter 5

The New Testament Church of God

The Church of God in England, generally referred to as the New Testament Church of God, has been said to be the most dynamic of all the black church groups operated by West Indians in that country. Its story is fascinating and certainly moving. More than half of its pilgrimage is linked with the life of a West Indian minister from Jamaica.

Painful Beginnings and Consolidation 1951-1955

In 1951 a young minister seeking social betterment was deliberating whether he should migrate to Europe. It was not an easy decision. He didn't want to be out of the will of God. This young man was Oliver A. Lyseight. In September of 1951, he reluctanctly drove to the Manley Airport, wondering what God would say in all this travail. While waiting at the airport, he received a congratulating letter from a fellow pastor, urging him to go and minister to the Jamaican brethren who were waxing "cold" in England.

Lyseight arrived in England November 9, 1951. He settled in Wolverhampton where a small retinue of

Telling the Story

compatriots resided. They were not the best prospects for spiritual fellowship for this soul-searching minister, because they had already backslidden. For the next two years, Lyseight decided to worship with British Pentecostal churches until he could go on his own. In 1952 the McCarran-Walter Immigration Act was passed, which provided for a limited British/West Indian immigration to America. An annual quota of 800 was acceptable. As a result of this, a large scale West Indian immigration converged to England. With this new momentum in immigration, more Jamaicans started to arrive in the British Isles. At first Jamaicans chose to worship in the native churches, but were shocked by the low level of attendance by the British. Moreover, because they were black, they were not welcome even when they attended the same churches they were affiliated with in Jamaica. Facing the blunt of prejudice in foreign lands, they decided to establish their own fellowship.

Lyseight was grieved by the fact that the West Indians were like a sheep without a shepherd, so he and a friend rented a YMCA building in Wolverhampton and started a church with less than 10 people. In his own words, Lyseight recounts these small beginnings.

> We met with many rebuffs, and at first they were only seven of us who maintained the cause. But we started to fast and pray for God to give us a breakthrough. Sometimes we borrowed other Pentecostal churches on Saturday nights after their meetings and held prayer meetings until midnight.[1]

During the same period, another mission was started in Handsworth, Birmingham. In 1955 Paul H. Walker, executive director of World Missions, went to England and organized these two churches. The church at Wolverhampton had 25 members and Handsworth had 40. In March 1956 Reverend Ray Hughes came to conduct an evangelistic tour, but it had to be cancelled for lack of suitable facilities. In May of the same year, Lyseight was appointed national overseer of the church in England. The Church of God in England was set for expansion. Due to increasing immigration, the New Testament Church of God was blessed with other church workers from the islands, all fired up for evangelism. In 1957 seven missions were being operated in the United Kingdom.

The Evolution of the New Testament Church of God, 1956-1978

The Push for Expansion. Having pastored in Jamaica, Lyseight aggressively pushed for the expansion of the work in England. As the work grew, better facilities were needed. For years the church worshiped in rented halls. The first time this congregation ever worshiped in a sanctuary was when they rented a Baptist church in Hammersmith. In a sense, that they no longer needed to carry the ark—they had a tabernacle. A revolving fund was set to pool offerings and contributions from the churches for building purposes. Out of this fund, many congregations would be able to acquire their own places of worship.

Building a Better National Ministry. Because of the growth of the church, small sanctuaries could no longer accommodate the annual national conventions. The church needed a better venue for the thousands of delegates who flooded to these gatherings. Two men set out to find a place for the 1962 Annual Convention. As they explored the vicinity of George Street, they met a British parson who informed them that the Villa Methodist Church was for sale. This information was conveyed to the general leaders, who ultimately acquired the building. The purchase was providential because this church served as national headquarters and convention venues until 1976.

Education and Training

As young people started to join the movement, they demanded the attention of the church. To retain the young people, the Church of God hired a young Trinidadian, Reverend Selwyn Arnold, as national youth director in 1962. This appointment led the church to focus on education and training. At the National Youth Convention in 1962, delegates were moved by the idea of setting a permanent Bible school, and an offering was raised for this purpose. During the same year, the school was opened at 244 Lozells Road, Lozells, Birmingham with Dr. G. Fitzwarren Barnes as principal.

The New Testament Church of God Bible School was the first school not initiated by foreign missionaries to serve West Indians. Debuting with five full-time teachers and 20 students, this Bible school became a vital institution for the growth of both clergy and laity. The name was changed to Ebenezer Bible Institute when it finally provided full-time training and reported a total enrollment of 10. The school was supported primarily through offerings, fees and grants from Church of God World Missions and it held its first graduation ceremonies in 1965. After five years of operation, the day school was discontinued due to the lack of funds. The students were encouraged to attend the European Bible School in Switzerland. Ebenezer Bible College survived, however, as an evening Bible Institute.

In 1976 the ministers meeting in National Conference voted to open an extension of the Bible Institute to accommodate the educational needs of the membership scattered in the southern section of London. A year later, another Bible evening institute was inaugurated in Hackney in the basement of the Clapton Church. Ira Brooks was the principal, and 90 students enrolled in this new program.

While a structure for education was being established, the youth ministry was also being consolidated. The Youth Department organized its first National Youth Seminar at the Handsworth Church in January 1966. After the Arnolds left for Africa, William Bucknor served as national youth director and was responsible for the organization of the first National Youth Camp in Cloverley Hall, Whitchurch Stropshire with 35 delegates. Efforts to establish a national program of education was vigorously pursued in 1976, and in 1979 the Youth Department combined with the European Youth Department.

The New Testament Church of God Since 1978

After 27 years at the helm, Lyseight resigned and the Reverend Jeremiah McIntyre, a loyal minister, was installed as the next overseer. By then the church was no longer erring in the wilderness; it had reached Canaan and the people were praising God in comfortable temples formerly occupied by Methodists, Catholics and Anglicans.

Jeremiah McIntyre from Jamaica was born in 1931,

Telling the Story

called to ministry in 1943 and licensed in 1953. He held various pastorates in his homeland in Lucea, Richmond, and Retrieve, Hanover, and in Sherwood and Perthtown, Trelawny. Pastor McIntyre decided to move to England in 1956, where he would pastor for 20 years. In the United Kingdom, he aggressively pushed for evangelism and was instrumental in planting churches in Balsall Heath, Crewe, Bolston, Preston, Oldham, Liverpool and Southampton. In 1976 he migrated to Canada where he served as coordinator for the French and English churches during 1976-1978. While living in Canada, he opened congregations in Ottawa and Montreal.

Appointed to the leadership of the New Testament Church of God in 1978, McIntyre was to remain in that position for eight years. Having studied at the University of London, C.O.F.I., and the International Bible Seminary, he was grounded in education and burdened for a better ministerial training program. As a matter of fact, he would later consider the milestone of his administration to be the acquisition of Overstone, a Victorian mansion with 107 rooms, which would house the Bible College.

As the church in England continued, it again outgrew existing meeting facilities, and the leadership had to locate another venue for the annual conventions. McIntyre advertised and had to reject several offers because the properties were inconveniently located. He visited Overstone and knew it was what God wanted them to have. Overstone was purchased in 1980 for $308,000 and renovated at a cost of $615,583. It has served the church since as national headquarters, parsonage for the national overseer and national director of education, and instructional facilities. The acquisition of this former manor per-

permitted the consolidation of the two Bible Institute programs and provided a convenient venue for Overstone Bible College, which opened in 1982. Ridley N. Usherwood was named as director and 57 students enrolled. It has been used for ministerial retreats, church retreats, regional Bible school and Step Program activities.

In 1984, Dr. Selwyn Arnold replaced Reverend McIntyre as overseer of England and Wales and led the church to pioneer a Social Ministry Department in 1986. Arnold Kirlew was the first director of the Social Ministry Department, which included a senior citizens' center, a youth club and a recreational program for children under 5 years old. The New Testament Church of God received a major grant of $440,000 for the renovation of the Bible College. In 1992 Dr. Arnold was succeeded by Reverend Ronald Brown as leader of the New Testament Church of God.

The New Testament Church of God has received several distinctions. One of which was to have one of its constituents to be elected as the leader of the Evangelical Alliance, a network of 3,000 local congregations. In 1988, Joel Edwards of Jamaica became general secretary of the African Caribbean Evangelical Alliance. Four years later, Reverend Edwards was pointed as director of the Evangelical Alliance, which has 55,000 members, 700 societies, 3,000 local churches and 300 Pentecostal congregations. Since 1992 Edwards has been serving on the National Executive Council of the Church of God in England. His objective for the church in the United Kingdom is to help it transform into a "Biblical Christianity increasingly emerging as credible and relevant in the British context and with a commitment to be a part of the wider Christian community."[2]

Causes of Growth

The evangelistic fervor of the West Indians accounts for much of their success in evangelism and church planting. After all, many of them were affiliated with the Church of God in their homeland, where they had developed soul-winning skills. The use of mother congregations was put to use in England. The church in Willesden served as a sponsor congregation for churches in Cricklewood, Stoke, Newington, Holloway and Horsey. The church at Brixton mentored the churches at Catford, Greenwich, Woolwich, Clapham, Deptford, Croydon, Mile End and Thornton Heath. Several of the ministers who went to the British Isles became seasoned church planters. There was an abundance of soul harvesters—G. S. Peddie, H.D. Brown, and S.U. Thompson were among the pioneers. Pastors Felix Poyser, Ronald Brown, Curtis Grey, Isaiah Campbell and Jeremiah McIntyre, all worked as church planters in the United Kingdom. Through their efforts the Church of God finally entered Cardiff, Wales. Being full-fledged Pentecostals, these believers also preached divine healing and miracles. At the church of Handsworth, one blind person was completely healed, and in another church, a woman pronounced dead was raised to life again in the name of the Lord.

> On one occasion at the church in Crewe, a sister took ill and was admitted into Hospital. After being taken there, the doctors could not help her, and after being here, they pronounced her dead, and sent to inform her

husband. When he and some brethren got there she was already laid out in the mortuary, but they fell down desperately on their knees beside where she was laid, and began to pray in one accord. When they were through praying, she was awakened—she was alive! The nurses and doctors were astonished, and from thence the Hospital Staff called her the miracle woman.[3]

The Church of God in England became the "home church" for hundreds of West Indian Christians, since they were not welcome in British churches. Many non-Pentecostal Christians affiliated with the mainline churches back home defected to the New Testament Church of God. The Church of God supported this growth and assisted in the acquisition of proper places of worship.

Chapter 6

Ethnic Growth

As of today, the Church of God is the only white Pentecostal denomination in North America with a significant black constituency. This growth among minorities in the church has not resulted without careful planning and sacrifices. Bureaucratic decisions, as well as institutional components, have impacted this burgeoning progress of the Church of God. Above all polity, innovation, emphasis on ethnic evangelism and visionary state leadership have set the tone for continuous growth.

Episcopal Polity and Innovativeness

Unlike some other Pentecostal bodies, the Church of God maintains a centralized form of government; individuals are responsible for the implementation of all major decisions. This system can be negative or positive. In an Episcopal system, executive leaders can destroy an organization through unwise decisions. Since they exercise a great deal of power, there is always the possibility that their decisions can hinder the growth of their administration. On the other hand, creative leaders in this kind of polity can set the pace

Telling the Story

by seeing that new ideas are implemented. Since the mid-'60s, the Church of God has been honored to have people who had a vision for urban growth. In 1961, the church decided to hire a full-time director for the newly created Department of Evangelism and Home Missions. Until World War II, the Church of God was mostly rural. In 1965 General Overseer Wade Horton led his denomination to adopt a program of metropolitan evangelism. This effort to target the cities was also intended to reach immigrants and had an impact on the African-American church. Since the end of World War II, thousands of black Americans have moved from the agrarian South to the booming cities of the North.

In the '70s, the evangelistic thrust was led by Dr. Ray H. Hughes, an acclaimed preacher. Burning with evangelistic fervor, Hughes worked out a program of total evangelism in 1972. One year later, the Big Brother-Little Brother program was developed, which assisted weak states financially and allowed them to do more in the area of church planting. This program took four years to reach its potential, and then it doubled within two years. The strategy was to organize one church a day. During the next decade, all general leaders emphasized the need for church planting. What were the results of this evangelistic challenge of the '70s? Between 1973 and 1978, the church organized more than 365 congregations a year.

Emphasis on Ethnic Evangelism

With the creation of the Department of Evangelism and Home Missions, the church started to develop new structures to reap the urban harvest. Since the harvest was multifaceted, diverse means and people were employed.

Ethnic Growth

In order to meet the needs of the ethnic harvest, the Executive Committee appointed J.D. Golden, then serving as overseer of New York-Metro, as the first director of the newly-created Cross-Cultural Ministries in 1980. Two years later, Billy Rayburn (from Illinois) replaced him and became the first full-time director of the office. Again, it was envisioned that this agency would focus on the promotion of the Church of God among the ethnic communities of the United States and Canada. In a 1982 interview, Rayburn spelled out the burden of his office. "The Cross-Cultural Ministry has been established to meet the ongoing need of providing the benefits of the church and her ministries to the millions who have come to the United States and Canada and to those who will come in the future."[1]

Cross-Cultural Ministries takes very seriously the business of ethnic evangelism. In 1987, it sponsored a major seminar on cross-cultural ministries at the Church of God Theological Seminary. This seminar reflected the continuous diffusion of the principles of the Church Growth Movement within the Church of God. Another important decision was the appointment of 25 cross-cultural consultants in 1991. This consulting body was "to provide information from the field, as well as offering ideas and suggestions for cross-cultural ministry opportunities."[2]

Cross-Cultural Ministries also offered a helping hand to congregations planning to set up a new churches. According to this department, at least one-third of ethnic church groups have been helped in property acquisitions. To promote its vision among the larger constituency, the ethnic office has already published two books on cross-cultural ministry: *Reaching Urban Ethnics* and *Planting Churches Cross-Culturally.*

Visionary State Leadership

The history of the church in the latter half of the century cannot be written without mentioning the involvement of the state overseers. Though plans come out of Cleveland, Tennessee, it is the overseers who are really the footmen. In trying to meet the ethnic challenge, no one could be more influential than those at the middle level of management. In New York, Florida, and Illinois among other places, overseers were the creative link in making breakthroughs in evangelism.

As far as New York is concerned, the key figures in the growth of the black work at all levels were J.D. Golden and Phil Higgins. Golden's personal biography highlights any dictionary of Christianity. Born in Alabama, Golden dug out his first church in Chicago, which later became the largest in the state. Because of his record as a pastor, he was tapped by his superiors to be the first evangelist of Chicago Metro. As evangelist, he organized churches in Wisconsin, Indiana and Illinois. In 1972 the Church of God appointed him to be the next overseer of New York. This New York assignment catapulted this southern preacher into national prominence. During his overseership, the number of congregations grew from 10 to 75 and the membership from 410 to 6,000.

Golden's ministry was primarily ethnic. Hispanic, West Indian and Asian congregations mushroomed under his leadership. Because of his original work in New York, he was called to participate in the National Convocation on Evangelizing Ethnic America in April

Ethnic Growth

1985. His leadership was much appreciated by the Lausanne Covenant Committee and by denominational leaders and church growth experts such as Peter C. Wagner, who attended this historic conference.

What was so revolutionary about Golden's ministry? He put into operation the following concepts and practices.

Ethnic District and Leaders. In Acts 6:1-7, a complaint arose from the Grecian widows. The leaders of the church decided to appoint Jewish men of Greek background to handle the problem. From this precedent, it is clear that the New Testament seems to be in favor of ethnic people ruling their own. But it was not just a knowledge of the Bible that moved Golden to commit himself to ethnic work—it was a personal conviction. Reminiscing about his Chicagoan ministry 20 years later, Golden said God opened his eyes as to the great scope of His harvest.

> While I was serving as Metro Evangelist in the Chicago area, the Lord awakened me one night and dealt with me about my ministry. He let me know that he would bless whom he desired to bless. I was to bless those whom God blessed. Weeping before God, I repented of my limited vision of the harvest and promised God that I would bless whomever he wanted blessed. That experience changed my life and my ministry.[3]

With this new vision, Golden became the Church of God champion and a national expert on ethnic growth across America.

> Soon, God allowed me to serve in New York City.

Telling the Story

> The work in New York City increased dramatically because we adjusted our thinking, left the old geographical district method, and established cultural districts that fully utilized the abilities of our ethnic ministers.[4]

This practice of geographic district was hindering progress, because churches were grouped together under an Anglo district overseer, regardless of origins and culture. Many aspects of foreign cultures could not be perceived by the regular leaders, even though they could speak the language of such immigrants as the British West Indians. To promote growth, Golden created Jamaican and Haitian districts. Peter Gayle and Honore Jacques, from Jamaica and Haiti respectively, filled these positions. This system worked and Gayle would later be credited with planting 15 churches. Honore Jacques was instrumental in pioneering more than 25 congregations in New York alone.

Skyscraper Evangelism. We all have heard that tract witnessing is an easy way to reach people for the kingdom of God. It may work well for some, but not necessarily in New York City. Thousands of New Yorkers live in high-rise buildings, and they would not want you to come to their 20th floor and knock on their doors to give out tracts.

In New York City, Golden commissioned what he called "skyscraper missionaries." He would place Church of God families in high-rise buildings for the purpose of evangelism. As these "missionaries" settled in, they gained freedom to knock on doors and witness to people. Not asking to do less, ethnic soul winners, sponsored by the New York State Office, won people to

Ethnic Growth

the Lord as skyscraper missionaries. These newly converted people became cells out of which churches were organized. This is metro evangelism.

Property Sharing and Acquisitions. The Big Apple is well known to carry unbelievable high real estate costs. As congregations grew, it became quite clear that larger facilities were needed. Due to the scarcity of facilities, congregations were like the Israelites in the wilderness. Most of the members were facing economic hardships and could contribute only so much to building funds. It is reported that one congregation was evicted seven times by the city for nonpayment of rent.

In 1978 a four-story building was bought through the YWEA program and shared simultaneously by multiple ethnic congregations. It was called the International Church. Eventually, these congregations were able to move out on their own. They grew in membership and in tithes, and many became the largest churches in the state. Such was the case for the East Flatbush Church of God and the Cortelyou Road Church of God in Brooklyn, New York.

Had this effort not been made, these congregations would have dwindled, and perhaps the most affluent members would have gone elsewhere. Golden held his first state convention in a funeral home chapel. Eight years later, it was held in a section of Madison Square Garden. The church was triumphant.

Transportation. Since many immigrants were of the working class, they could not afford to travel to church. Even some of the ethnic ministers did not have cars. This generated a retention problem. It is well known by

Telling the Story

church growth experts that lack of personal participation usually translates into apathy and disaffection. Golden tackled this problem of transportation, and by 1977 one-half of the ethnic churches had bus ministries.

In 1987 Gene Rice, state overseer of Florida, made a visionary decision when he hired a full-time cross-cultural director. Though Pastor Marvin Johnson was working with the blacks, Earl Cushman, the first director of ethnic ministries in Florida, was able to expand the work.

Chapter 7
Jamaican and Haitian Congregations

The West Indian Church of God in the United States was not born out of evangelistic campaigns—it came out of the inflow of believers from the Caribbean into North America. In 1965 the Hart-Celler Immigration Act abolished quotas and triggered a large-scale West Indian immigration to the United States.

Laying the Foundations

In 1957 Peter Barrett, a Jamaican minister, went to England. He and his wife, Daphne, were instrumental in founding a new congregation in Croydon. During a visit to the States in 1962, Barrett visited Hartford, Connecticut, and learned that there was no Jamaican Church of God in the city. He went back to England, resigned his pastorate and returned to North America. He explored Toronto in 1963 and then evangelized in Buffalo, New York, hoping to minister both in Buffalo and nearby Toronto. Later he settled in Hartford, Connecticut, and started a prayer meeting with three people. According to our records, that was the first Jamaican congregation in the States. In November 1968 Clifford McDonald from Jamaica started another

Telling the Story

congregation in Toronto, Canada. The Jamaican Church of God was moving.

Peter Barrett was involved in church planting and helped quite a few ministers from England settle in this country. He has since gone to be with the Lord, but Blue Hills Church of God, which he pastored in Connecticut, remains as a living testimony of his labors.

The Growth of the Jamaican Church of God

One key figure in later growth of Jamaican churches in America was the Reverend Peter Gayle. In the early '70s, he served for some time as assistant pastor to Guy Notice, founder of what is now the East Flatbush Church of God in Brooklyn, New York. Two years later, Gayle became the senior pastor of this growing congregation. The church is still considered to be one of the largest black Church of God congregations in America. They seat 700 people every Sunday and their facilities are valued at more than $1 million.

The East Flatbush Church of God was founded in 1970 by the Reverend Guy Notice. In 1974 Notice was appointed principal of the Bethel Bible College in Jamaica. Gayle, his assistant, assumed the leadership of this fledging congregation. Like all who move to a new position, he went through adjustment problems, but God had a way out for him.

> During the first two years I served as pastor, 95 percent of the people did not accept me. This made it very difficult. However, I called the people to three days of fasting. And God gave the victory.[1]

Jamaican and Haitian Congregations

Pastor Gayle used two means to encourage growth in his church: involvement and community pastoring. On the first Sunday of each month, the young people, who accounted for almost half of the congregation, were in charge of the morning and evening services. They usually provided the speakers from among their own. On the second Sundays, women were responsible for the worship service. On the third Sundays, the Men's Fellowship made their own contribution to the devotional and spiritual life of the church. Another of Gayle's assets was the ability to skillfully deploy the membership. He was not a "superpastor," blessed with all the gifts of the Spirit at once. He said, "I am not afraid of delegating authority and responsibility to various individuals, expecting them to do their job and report to me on a regular basis."[2] Three associate ministers worked with him and relieved him of the anxiety of dealing with hundreds of people alone.

The ministry of this congregation is staunchly Pentecostal. Because of their faith in healing, they have seen the glory of God. In the '70s, the senior pastor was facing death, due to a damaged heart and an overactive thyroid. The congregation prayed and he was healed. Mrs. Emeline Gayle had cancer that, thanks to the Lord, was not fatal. Gayle experienced other miracles such as the following:

> We saw God heal a young man with decayed kidneys. The doctors told him the only thing that would save him was a transplant or be on a dialysis machine the rest of his life. God healed him, and he did not have a transplant nor was put on a dialysis machine. The doctors marveled![3]

Telling the Story

From 1972 to 1987 the membership of this church grew from 50 to 1,500. Reverend Gayle was never limited in his vision for the hurting. As Wesley considered the world to be his parish, Gayle took Brooklyn as his parish.

> In times of death and bereavement the family needs somebody who cares. As a minister in this community, I want the people to know that I am their minister—not just the minister of the East Flatbush Church of God but the minister of this community for people who don't have a church home.[4]

This cosmopolitan perspective has much to do with church growth. As Gayle volunteered to officiate at the funerals of people in the community, many of the families of the deceased decided to join his congregation. This was John 17 in application. The practice of Christian love by real Christian people brings people to the kingdom of God. East Flatbush also witnessed to people through an evangelistic group that distributed 10,000 tracts monthly.

Gayle's importance in the growth of the black church is not circumscribed to his work as a local pastor. He contributed to the expansion of the Church of God in New York by assisting other ministers in planting their own congregations. Under J.D. Golden's leadership, he was made district overseer of a black district, putting him in a position to further encourage growth. In 1977 the East Flatbush Church of God planted three churches. By 1988 a total of nine churches were birthed from it. By 1994 Pastor Gayle had organized 15 churches in the New York-Metro Area. These baby congregations were fully

Jamaican and Haitian Congregations

supported by the mother congregation. When he retired in 1994, he was replaced by Dr. Lindsay Arscott, a graduate of the Church of God Theological Seminary.

New York is not the only state in which the Church of God has Jamaican congregations. All over Florida and southern New England, Jamaicans from England and the Caribbean have organized their own ministries. In Florida today, they are more than 10 Jamaican congregations. Two of them were pioneered by the Reverend Guy Notice. Isaiah Campbell was a key agent to the Jamaican growth in Florida. Campbell, a graduate of the Church of God Theological Seminary, has trained scores of pastors who went on to plant their own congregations. A significant ministry is still maintained in Perrine, Florida, by Pastor Walden, whose congregation has been able to build its own sanctuary after worshiping in a park in its "wilderness days."

In the Northeast Pastor Cecil Mullins, a member of the General of Evangelism and Home Missions, leads Mount Bethel Church of God, a vibrant congregation in Trenton, New Jersey. He is also a former president of the Northeast Regional Fellowship. In Dorchester, Massachusetts, Sister Rosena Davids has maintained a viable ministry.

In Pennsylvania, worth mentioning is Pastor Felix Poyser, district overseer, who started his ministry in England and contributed to the great evangelistic thrust in the British Isles. He has built from scratch a ministry which is the strongest Jamaican outreach in the Keystone State. Pastor Poyser is a former state council member, and in the eighties, organized various Bible enrichment seminars which were a blessing to the people of the Westside district. He has been instrumental in the planting of two other Jamaican ministries led by Pastors Jabez Barrett and Audley Thompson. Several auxiliary ministries have been developed by his congregation such as a nursing home ministry to the shut-in.

Overall, these immigrants from the former British West Indies have greatly supported the Regional Fellowships organized in the United States.

The Haitian Church of God

In the mid-'60s, the Reverend Honore Jacques moved to the United States and with 70 people, opened the first Haitian church of God in Brooklyn, New York. In 1973, Pastor Flaureste St. Fleur planted the first Haitian congregation in Montreal, Canada. These men laid the foundations. The Haitian work barely grew in the early '70s. It was to flourish in the mid-'70s as thousand of immigrants settled in large cities such as Brooklyn, New York, Miami, and Boston.

Reverend Georges Morrissett replaced Flaureste St. Fleur as regional coordinator of all the Haitian churches in Quebec, Montreal. Georges also supervises the Ministerial Internship Program (MIP) which prepares future ministers for the harvest.

This ethnic work today reports 91 Haitian congregations in the United States and 15 in Canada. Areas where the Haitian church is strong are New York, southern New England and Florida.

The Haitian Church of God in New York

Much of the history of the Haitian church is closely associated with the ministry of Dr. Honore Jacques and

Jamaican and Haitian Congregations

other prominent Haitian leaders. When Pastor Jacques moved to New York, little did he know that he would pioneer the entire Haitian program of the Church of God in the United States. For years the Haitian work dragged on and did not report significant growth until 1974, when a Haitian district was organized. It was revolutionary. Until then, the church had remained committed to the geographical districts, which were not especially helpful for ethnic church growth. This position gave Pastor Jacques more freedom to operate among his people and fulfill the plan of God.

> The Holy Ghost has always confirmed His work to me in clear visions. In one vision, God sent me to pray for Sister Jacqueline Joseph, a lady we had not seen for years. A few months later, she offered her home to start a mission. We began with twelve persons. News spread about the coming church and people gathered.[5]

Between 1972 and 1978, seven new ethnic congregations sprouted in the Big Apple. Because of the growth of the work, four new Haitian districts were created to nurture a greater fellowship level. Because of Jacques efforts, the Church of God has made tremendous gains among the Haitians in New York, and Canada. Between 1967 and 1992, the number of churches grew from one to 24 in New York.

If Paul had a vision for the Gentiles, John Knox a burden for Scotland, and Golden a dream for ethnic America, Reverend Jacques can be said to be more progressive about the Haitian harvest than anyone else. Not only has his congregation been a mother church for New

York, it was also instrumental in planting churches in southern New England, Florida and Canada.

The Haitian Church of God in New England

Honore Jacques is not the only church planter among the Haitians. Other effective planters are the Reverends Othon O. Noel, Eugene Germain, Joseph Noncent and Jean Vincent ministering in southern New England, New Jersey, Florida and Pennsylvania.

Dr. Othon Noel was born in Haiti and is a second-generation Church of God member. He studied both in Haiti and in Jamaica. In Haiti he ministered as evangelist, youth pastor, pastor, district overseer and pastor. In 1975 he visited Boston while en route to New York, where he planned to settle. During his four-week stay, he felt the leading of God to open an outreach in Boston. He returned to Boston in September 1975 and pioneered the first Haitian Church of God in his living room with eight people. Today this church worships with more than 500 every Sunday morning.

Like Pastor Gayle, Reverend Noel had a vision for his community. When his own church was only a year old, he began another church in the Somerville area. He wanted to take Boston for God. Indeed, early on Noel had sensed that God would make him a leader of his own people. While searching the will of God for his ministry, he received a divine revelation.

> I saw Jesus dressed in white and coming to me. He said, "Othon, Othon stand up and follow me." We walked many, many miles until we arrived in a city. He took me to the highest point of a castle, and from there I heard so much noise that I was afraid and stepped closer to Him.

Jamaican and Haitian Congregations

> Upon looking down I saw thousands and thousands of people—blind, deaf, diseased persons. He told me, "Do you see these people? You are responsible for them. Take care of them."[6]

With this commission from the Master in mind, he organized another Haitian group in Cambridge, Massachusetts. The next year, he began an English congregation in his own sanctuary. By 1981 he had started five churches. In 1987, 16 churches could trace their existence to Pastor Noel's congregation. The latest reports confirm that as of this year, Pastor Noel has assisted southern New England in organizing 25 churches since he moved to Massachusetts.

Reverend Noel clearly understood that he had to make his congregation pay the price for church planting. Dr. Polen recounting Noel's commitment to church planting commented in 1981.

> An example of his unselfish attitude and vision for growth is the Somerville (Haitian) Church, which he gave seventeen members and $700 a month tithes from his church in Dorchester. The Somerville church now has 54 members and paid $1,500 tithes in May 1981.[7]

The Haitian Church of God in Other Regions

In 1974, Eugene Germain moved from Guadeloupe to Miami to organize the first Haitian Church of God in Florida. He was instrumental in the development of the Haitian Church of God in that state. He helped many young ministers start their own congregations and has been called upon to serve as a representative of Haitian refugees before immigration authorities.

Telling the Story

His local congregation served as a center of evangelism for the Miami area. For 18 years the congregation met in a warehouse. As it grew they bought a larger building, which was renovated through the help of Men of Action.

Speaking of the burden of this Miami congregation, an article in the *Florida State News* made the following comment.

> Often arising at 5 a.m., the First Haitian Church gathered and called out to God to help them carry the gospel to their neighbors that number approximately 70,000. It has not been uncommon for this body of believers to pray past the noon hour, indicating their sincerity and zeal in fulfilling the great commission.[8]

To carry the Great Commission, Haitians in Miami have been greatly assisted by Anglo pastors who were willing to let them to use their church facilities. Pastors such as Walter Lauster, Joffre Vivoni, James Steele, Don Bishop, F. L. Braddock and Ken Houck have sheltered many of these congregations who now own their places of worship.

Joseph Noncent is the Haitian district overseer of New Jersey, where there are 14 Haitian congregations. As a church planter, Pastor Noncent has helped in digging out five of these churches and is responsible for 35 percent increase in churches.

A significant Pentecostal witness exists today in Pennsylvania though the First Haitian Church of God located in Philadelphia. It was founded in 1978 by the

Jamaican and Haitian Congregations

Reverends Jean and Marie Vincent, who moved to Pennsylvania from New York.

In late 1977, the Vincents were ministering in Manhattan, New York, when they received a call to come and pray with the Polche family in Philadelphia. In November of the same year, Reverend Vincent and his wife drove to the City of Brotherly Love and conducted the requested prayer service. At the time there were no other Pentecostal workers in the Haitian community there and interest soon began to spark. During the next three months, Pastor Vincent would make a two-hour drive from New York to Philadelphia to preach on Sunday afternoon for this nucleus of people. Sensing that the will of God for him was to minister permanently in the Keystone State, he put his house up for rent and moved to Philadelphia with a family of five, losing the opportunity to collect retirement annuities from a well-paying job.

District Overseer Robert Varner organized the church on Sunday, April 23, 1978, with 47 people. Varner has been a staunch supporter of the Haitian work, which he has assisted financially through all means possible. The church was first housed in a storefront. Later it acquired a former theater and refurbished it into a beautiful sanctuary. Today this church is a vibrant Pentecostal congregation that seats about 1,000. Recently, they inaugurated a Christian day school program and a day care center—a testimony in itself of the progressive spirit of its leadership. Because of his evangelistic vision, Pastor Vincent was able to plant five churches and two missions in the Keystone State.

Part 2

Biological Profiles

Chapter 8

Leadership in the Black Church

Ministry in the black church can take a variety of shapes depending on what you do and where you are. For 90 years, ministers have been in the forefront of the battle. This chapter will walk through some important figures of the past and present. Unfortunately, there are hundreds of hardworking leaders whose ministries are not surveyed here. May they appreciate their fellow ministers whose labors, described here, will inspire others.

For easy reference, the work of these ministers will be reviewed under these four chapters: Leadership, Evangelism, Social Concern and Education, and Missions.

John H. Curry (1894-1955)

Curry was born in 1894 in the Bahamas. He was saved in 1913 and migrated to Florida in 1914. He was called to the ministry in 1917 and licensed in 1920. Ordained in 1923, Curry was assigned the pastorate of the Miami Church in 1925 and later ministered to the Fort Lauderdale congregation. He served

Telling the Story

for some time as overseer of the East Coast district and was selected by S.W. Latimer to be the next national overseer of the black work upon the resignation of David LaFleur. Unlike any other black overseer, Curry was to serve in this position for 10 consecutive years.

Many things can be said of Bishop Curry. First, he was the one who materialized the dream of the African-Americans to erect an orphanage for poor children in 1934. Another memorable thing about him is that he was the one who envisioned the need to build an auditorium to hold the annual assemblies. After 1926 the conventions had been moving from city to city as these annual celebrations grew in attendance. At the Colored Assembly of 1929, it was agreed that the church would build an auditorium—preferably in Jacksonville, which was known as the gateway to Florida and the largest city in the state.

In 1936 the Jacksonville Auditorium was partially dedicated, and in 1954 the entire project was completed under Bishop Wallace. It has remained for a long time the glory of the black Pentecostals in Florida.

A third contribution of Curry was his dealing with the North/South problem in the colored work. In 1926, General Overseer Lee had granted the northern congregations the right not to affiliate with the black structure based in the South. Feeling that this initiative was hindering the progress of the black work, Curry strongly urged the general overseer to consolidate the entire black arm of the church.

This was effectively done in 1930. The major contribution of Curry was his emphasis on the need for an educated clergy. In 1931 a local Bible school was reportedly held in Florida. This was probably a first for the black work. At the Colored Assembly of 1932, Curry made a proposal that says a lot about his progressiveness.

> We are living in an educational era and the preparation of our ministers can not be stressed too much. All churches of any consequence have their seminaries for the training of those who are to preach and take care of the spiritual needs of the human family. This preparation enables them to render more helpful service in the community in which they domicile. Therefore, it is expedient at this time for me to inform you that ways and means must be devised by this conference to establish such an institution.[1]

To this groundbreaking invitation from their overseer, the Bishops' Council responded with the following:

> Seeing the necessity of a theological seminary for the purpose of preparing our ministers to intelligently cope with the Word, we do hereby recommend, that the sum of $150 be appropriated for said purpose. We suggest that the term of said school be held June, July, and August of each year in Jacksonville, Florida, and that the tuition be $5.00 a month of $15 a term. We recommend the Secretary-Treasurer as supervisor of said school. We further suggest, that each district select a student to send to the seminary and bear his scholastic expenses. This should be done for the express purpose of training teachers among our people.[2]

Because of this early concern, several local Bible schools have been held throughout the history of the black Church of God.

Telling the Story

The highlight of Curry's ministry was his appointment to serve on both the Council of Twelve (1932-1938) and the Council of Seventy (1926-1929). For six years he served on the former, and for three on the latter.

Peter Hickson (1902-1984)

Peter Hickson was born in South Carolina, the 14th child of George and Annah Hickson. Saved at the age of 6, he joined the Cypress Baptist Church. He later moved to Florida at the age of 10 and became involved in his local church as clerk and president of the youth organization. After his marriage to the former Hattie Bell Lott, he was ordained as a junior deacon. In Florida his wife received the experience of sanctification and then encouraged him to seek the same. While attending a revival preached by G. Sapp, Hickson received the Baptism of the Holy Spirit and set forth as clerk of the local Church of God—an offshoot of the same revival. Because of his abilities, he went on to fulfill several positions at the Eustis Church of God. Alternately, he was trustee, deacon, secretary-treasurer and Sunday school superintendent.

Influenced by Uriah P. Bronson, he accepted the position of district Sunday school superintendent and later assistant to the state superintendent for the Sunday school in Florida. In 1931, he became the president of the YPE in Florida, and the same year he was granted a pastorate in Umatilla, Florida.

Though Hickson wore several hats, it is as youth leader that he was to deploy all the resources of his talents. At the time, the youth work was poorly established in the black Church of God congregations. Only the state of Florida maintained a few youth organizations. Feeling

Leadership in the Black Church

a need for something bigger and better, Hickson took up upon himself the responsibility of establishing YPE in other states. At his own expense, he bought and sent literature to all the black churches and challenged them to organize a youth ministry.

One of the landmarks of Hickson's ministry was to organize the first YPE National Convention in 1932. This was reported to be then the biggest youth event of the entire black church up to that time. Delegates from 15 states or more flocked to the basement of the unfinished Jacksonville Auditorium. At this convention, the Bishops' Council elected Peter Hickson as general president of the entire YPE program of the black church. Vested with this authority, Hickson went on to deal with the urgent problems of his young constituency.

To provide the proper literature for the YPE, Hickson wrote to General Overseer Latimer in October 1932 and requested that the *Church of God Evangel* publish some relevant study helps tailored for young people. After much delay, a special issue was published on April 29, 1933, that carried 14 pages of printed literature for the YPE. It was a landmark for the young people. But Hickson was not satisfied. He needed something that would be continuous and not just a one-time effort.

In 1936 Hickson petitioned the Bishops' Council to start a paper in the interest of the YPE. On April 14, 1936, the Bishops' Council granted this request. But then there was the money problem. People were barely making a living after the Depression. But Hickson was a man of faith. The next day, he convened his YPE staff and appointed an editorial staff. After the adjournment of the General Assembly, Hickson prayed and sought

Telling the Story

God's direction as to what to do. It was finally decided that letters should be sent to all the churches.

A three-fold plan was also designed that called for three contests: one for the best name of the paper-to-be, another on the meaning of the new paper to the YPE, and the last one for the seller of the largest number of subscriptions. Mrs. B.M. Ballard from Pittsburgh, Pennsylvania was the winner of the first contest and the name "Church of God Gospel Herald" was adopted. The best article on the significance of the paper was written by Lula Mae Randolph from Eustis, Florida. Mrs. Essie Scott from Philadelphia, Pennsylvania sold the largest number of subscriptions.

By November 1936, Hickson had raised enough money to sustain the operation of the paper. On Sunday, November 29, 1936, the first issue of the *Church of God Gospel Herald* was published and all of the black churches held a special dedicatory service in its behalf.

Hickson went on to serve the church in many other capacities. For many years, he was the recording secretary and stenographer of the black assemblies. In 1947, he became the minister of the Jacksonville Church of God, and in 1958 he was appointed overseer of the Jacksonville district. After two years, he was moved to the Daytona Beach Church of God to the position of district overseer.

Peter Hickson served in many capacities in the church and is to be appreciated for having written and incorporated a history of the black church into the *Minutes of the 30th Annual Assembly of the Church of God Colored Work*. This rare document remains an invaluable source of information on the early years of the black work.

Leadership in the Black Church

Norbert S. Marcelle (1890-1969)

N.S. Marcelle of Fort Lauderdale, Florida, was born in 1890. After his salvation, he entered the ministry, was licensed in November 1923, and became ordained in June 1926. Marcelle served as district overseer under Bishop Curry and assisted him in his endeavors to upgrade the educational training of the ministry. As district overseer, he taught in several local Bible schools. He was made overseer over the Colored Work in 1938 and remained in this position until 1946. At the time of his episcopal appointment, the black church was heavily in debt, and Marcelle made it his concern to relieve the indebtedness on the Jacksonville Auditorium.

The nation was barely recovering from the Depression and life was difficult. The auditorium was partially completed and had been inaugurated in 1936, but it still had a balance of $1,541.74. Marcelle was successful in eliminating this debt by 1942. Some improvements were added to the building: a new roof was installed, and pews were added. Marcelle was also was concerned about the Orphanage. He completed the boys' dormitory. Under J.T. Roberts, Marcelle worked as overseer of New York and New Jersey and became superintendent of education in 1957. He has been followed in the ministry by his two sons, Charles and N.S. Marcelle Jr.

Willie L. Ford (1908-1987)

Willie Ford, of Evergreen, Alabama, was born in 1908. He entered the ministry in 1928 and was ordained in 1938. He was privileged to serve two terms as national overseer (1946-1950, 1954-1958). Experienced as district and state overseer, he had a business mind and was a careful administrator. He was responsible for two major accomplishments during his administration: the elimination of the debt on the Orphanage in 1948, and the organization of a national missions program in 1954. Bishop Ford is also noted to have promoted the continuous operation of the orphanage through a downsizing of personnel and an increase in educational costs.

George Wallace (1893-1976)

Wallace was educated in Nassau, Bahamas, and maintained a progressive spirit. He was ordained in 1929, and pastored in Jensen, Hallandale and Fort Pierce. Under Curry, he taught various local Bible schools. He was an original member of the Bishops' Council, which was instituted in 1930. He was an accomplished musician, choir director and music teacher. In 1950, he was elected to be national overseer and made history with his determination to see the completion of Jacksonville Auditorium in 1954.

Oliver A. Lyseight

Oliver A. Lyseight was born in Jamaica in 1920, and was the eldest child of his family. He was raised in Claremont, Hanover, and lost his father at the age of 4. In his adolescent years, he assumed the financial responsibility for his family. As a boy, he always wanted to be a preacher. He was saved at the age of 8 in the Methodist church and three years later joined the Church of God. He served as Sunday school teacher and superintendent and was later licensed as a minister. During World War II, he worked in the United States for the War Food Service and later returned to his native land. There, he served four pastorates.

In early 1951, he reluctantly decided to go to England. He received assurance that he was in the will of the God only when he reached the airport. After a stop in New York, Lyseight finally reached England in November 1951 after winning converts in transit. For two years, he preached in British churches before going on his own. With the flow of immigrants reaching England, he and a group of devout Pentecostals rented a hall and started to preach the gospel. In 1955, two congregations were organized by the Reverend Paul H. Walker, executive secretary of World Missions. This was the beginning of the New Testament Church of God in the motherland of the British Empire. In 1956 Lyseight was appointed to the overseership of the church in England. The rest is history. In 1978 Lyseight resigned as national overseer, and was later granted a honorary doctor of divinity by Lee University.

At the time of his resignation, the New Testament Church of God claimed 5,000 members, 87 churches, 8 missions and 191 ministers. Without doubt, Lyseight was one of these men who were called for "such a time as this."

Several important personality characteristics of this leader were instrumental in shaping the destiny of the British work. First, there was a sense of destiny. Reminiscing on the early beginnings, he commented: "I was often homesick . . . but I knew God had a greater purpose in my coming to England than to find a good job. Little did I know what he had in mind."[3] Even in Jamaica he had already anticipated somewhat what will happen later in his life overseas.

Telling the Story

> My first vision was in my home in Jamaica, just a few months after conversion, when I had (sic) Isaiah 6:8-10, at a time I started preaching, I had visions of strange Country. I saw double-decker buses, when I never even knew that such things existed anywhere. Then the time came, and it was so ... God showed me some of the success and even failure in the ministry at different intervals. So I was always aware of some of the happenings.[4]

A second element to be recalled is his strong faith. He was undaunted by obstacles and trusted God to provide for new properties, even when there were no funds available or when bankers were political and verbose in denying loan applications. He didn't take "no" for an answer and utilized negative answers to teach bankers about the meaning of faith. The result? Bankers consulted their bosses and approved loans of at least 8,000 pounds. This explained in part how 40 church buildings were bought by 1978. As a preacher, Lyseight was bold and showed no respect of persons. While ministering in Wolverhampton, he met uneasy natives asking why a new "society" was needed when there were many empty churches in the land. He used this opportunity to denounce the sinful practices of some of the members of those churches and their ministers. He was a black replica of John Knox, the fiery Scottish preacher.

Early on, Lyseight maintained a strong evangelistic push. At the very first Minister's Conference, plans were already made for new field evangelism. Parks and street corners were used and canvassed to rescue the lost. During those wilderness years, the church did house-to-house visitations, handed out tracts and kept themselves aflame through all-night prayer meetings. They went to the hedges and the highways.

When the church had to face the harsh reality of the need for permanent facilities, Lyseight showed his organizational skills by developing a "revolving fund." This was a sort of cooperative pool savings that allowed the churches to make contributions for a national building fund. Buildings were the chief setbacks, but the earth was the Lord's.

Because of his strong personality, Lyseight was able to deafen criticisms and move on with the work of God. His concern for progress led him to engineer with Reverend Selwyn Arnold what is now Overstone Bible College. From this school dozens of graduates have gone on to serve the Lord in Canada, Africa, the United States and other countries. Looking to reach the harvest, Pastor Lyseight helped the Church of God to enter Pakistan, Liberia and Ghana. A community person, he was involved in civic associations such as the Wolverhampton Employment Panel, the Wolverhampton Education Authority and the Wolverhampton Commission for Racial Equality. A high point of his ministry was to be invited to speak at the 10th World Pentecostal Conference in Seoul, Korea.

Reflecting on his overseership, Lyseight considered the acquisition of properties, a National Office, a Bible school and thousands of converts to be his crowning achievements. No wonder that a director of World Missions addressed him with the words.

> I am sure that the great work that God has developed under your care is a constant source of satisfaction and joy to you. I also know that the greatest reward of all

awaits you when the Lord himself declares you "that good and faithful servant" and invites you to enter into the "joys of the Lord."[5]

Goodwin Smith

Goodwin Smith is one of the few leaders of the Church of God who has been privileged to serve on both the Executive Council (1986-1990, 1996-present) and the World Missions Board (1982-1990). Dr. Smith has evangelized extensively in the Caribbean and has also ministered in Germany, England and the Netherlands, and was a speaker at the 1980 General Assembly.

Dr. Smith's early exposure to the gospel was through the United Holiness Church of America and the African Methodist Episcopal Church. Born in Bermuda, the young Smith migrated to the United States in 1968, and later earned the doctor of divinity degree. He settled in Brooklyn, New York and served the pastorate of the 117th Street Church of God for six years. In 1974 he returned to Bermuda and was appointed national overseer. He now pastors the Union and Dundonald Street New Testament Church of God in Hamilton, Bermuda.

Dr. Smith is very active in community affairs, and has been president of the Bermuda Pentecostal Fellowship and Bermuda Ministerial Association, member of the Inter-City Board on the Minsuse of Drugs (a government appointment). Reverend Smith was chosen by the Governor of Bermuda to serve as a member of the Human Rights Board of Inquiry. In 1988 Dr. Smith was bestowed the distinguished honor of becoming a Member of the British Empire (M.B.E.) by Queen Elizabeth II of England.

Chapter 9

More Outstanding Evangelists

It was discovered early on the history of the black Pentecostals that when it came to evangelists, the congregations preferred one of their own race. Black evangelists covered the country, winning souls for Christ. It would take an entire book to tell of all the great black evangelists. In this chapter, we will mention just a few.

Calvin C. Daniels

C.C. Daniels is one of the longest serving minister in the Church of God. He has been pastoring for more than 50 years.

Reverend Daniels was born on January 8, 1929. His mother was a church clerk, his father a deacon and his uncle a minister. He enrolled in the service and went to the Korean War. When he was discharged from the Army, he felt a call to the ministry and started a church in his home state, which already had four congregations.

In those years there were other denominations in the South and the black work experienced several

Telling the Story

defections. Pastor Daniels vividly recalls having been sent by the Lord to one of churches where he told the congregation to beware of "wolves in sheep's clothing." This particular congregation later confessed that it was about to leave the Church of God for another denomination. Because of the preaching of this man, that church did not leave. In 1957 Daniels was appointed overseer of Mississippi by J.T. Roberts. For 13 years, Reverend Daniels served as overseer and planted three churches. In 1966 the Church of God dissolved the national structure of the black work, but Mississippi remained segregated until the 1970 General Assembly, which finally dissolved the black judicatory.

When Wallace Sibley became regional director of evangelism, Brother Daniels worked with him and was instrumental in calling the Mississippi Black Fellowship Conference in 1979.Today, there are nine black churches in Mississippi that have been planted under the care of Bishop Daniels.

Last July, the Black Ministries Department organized an appreciation service for Pastor Daniels to celebrate his more than 40 years in the ministry. Dr. Dennis McGuire, liaison to Black Ministries, was the guest speaker.

Willie C. Menendez

W.C. Menendez is one of those pioneers of metro evangelism in the Church of God in the modern era. He is the son of Blanche Menendez, a devout woman who was formerly a Baptist. Since she joined the Church of God, Sister Menendez has made herself a valuable member and has served in several roles in her local church.

More Outstanding Evangelists

W.C. Menendez was born in 1925. He was raised in a Church of God family and entered the Christian ministry in 1948. He was licensed in 1952 and has been a pastor, evangelist and overseer of the black churches of New Jersey under J.T. Roberts. His church-planting ministry was effective, and he was able to organize five new congregations while in New Jersey. After the integration of the church, Menendez became district overseer and was elected to the state council of New Jersey. In January 1968, he resigned his pastorate in Freehold and accepted a position to work under Walter Pettitt, as missionary and metro evangelist. That was a time when the Church of God was pushing for urban evangelism, and Menendez was deployed to reach urban blacks. He preached in Florida, Maryland and Alabama, where he dug out a church in Pritchard in January 1971. In 1974 Menendez was chosen to be overseer of Florida, a position he filled for four years. He organized 32 successful district and youth conventions in Florida and 11 Florida Bible Institutes.

Willie Vaughn

In December 1974, the state councils of Oregon and Washington met in joint session and considered the issue of combining the ethnic work of the Northwest. It was finally resolved that there was a need for a director of cross-cultural affairs. With the blessing of the Executive Committee, they looked for the right man and appointed Reverend Willie Vaughn as director of metro ethnic affairs for Washington and Oregon. The work of this preacher can be read as a classic example of apostolic church planting.

Telling the Story

Before his appointment, Vaughn was pastor of the Pasco Church of God and had already worked with the state evangelism director of Washington in the capacity of director of ethnic affairs for the state of Washington. Living in an area where the Church of God had a limited witness, Vaughn approached the problem of church planting from the grassroots. With a lack of available workers, Vaughn started from scratch, roaming the cities, trying to win, not church-affiliated people, but those who had not met the Lord. When he had a sufficient number of people, then the state overseer would call for pastors from elsewhere to come and lead these new converts. Overseer Brinson reported his hard work in the state of Washington.

> Brother Vaughn dug out a church in central Seattle which now has its own pastor and fine worship facilities. Brother Vaughn accomplished this while continuing to pastor the Pasco Church and while driving 220 miles one way to walk the streets of Seattle and knock on doors.[1]

Using this kind of techniques, Vaughn was successful in organizing 13 churches in the Northwest. Another milestone of his ministry was initiating a new level of fellowship among the ethnic groups and allowing more young black people to identify with the Church of God. In his own words, he stated, "The purpose of the fellowship was to mobilize and acquaint people with the Church of God and to strengthen those who were already members of the body."[2] Sensing that the young people did not have a forum for fellowship, he pioneered the Northwest Pentecostal Fellowship in 1975, which still meets every year.

Honore Jacques

Dr. Honore Jacques from Haiti was used by God to plant at least one-third of the 116 Haitian congregations in the United States and Canada.

He was born 1938 into a Catholic family and served as an altar boy. While attending a baptism, he was pricked in his heart and surrendered himself to the Lord. At the age of 19 he began to preach and then entered the Church of God Bible School. He served two pastorates in Haiti and later migrated to the United States.

In 1967 Jacques opened a church in Brooklyn, New York, that was to become the mother congregation for many other new churches. In 1969 another congregation was set forth in Nyack, New York. In 1972 J.D. Golden came to New York as state overseer, and for two years, growth remained slow. In 1974 Pastor Jacques approached Golden about his vision for the Haitian work, and in that year Reverend Jacques was made district overseer of the Haitian congregations. In 1978 Golden appointed Jacques coordinator of the Haitian work in New York Metro, where there were four Haitian districts. In 1978 they were 20 Haitian congregations in America. Twenty years later, they had grown to no less than 116 congregations in both the US and Canada. While immigration fueled church planting in Florida in the late '80s, Reverend Jacques laid the foundations for the expansion of the church across North America. His involvements were many.

Telling the Story

First of all, he served as interpreter for the new migrant ministers and linked them to the denomination in America. He encouraged ministers coming from Haiti to renew their fellowship with the Church of God in the states. He also encouraged those ministers to plant their own congregations. Reverend Flaureste St. Fleur from Haiti moved to Canada in 1973 and was advised to open a congregation there. In 1974 Honore Jacques linked with Reverend Germain who was led to take over a work in Miami, Florida. Today, there are more than 25 Haitian churches in Florida. Dr. Othon Noel, who pastors in Massachusetts, served under Reverend Jacques and was sponsored by him and J.D. Golden in southern New England in 1975. Noel had already planted 25 congregations in southern New England. Pastor Jacques not only advised immigrant ministers from Haiti, but he also encouraged young trailblazers to enter the ministry. Many lay people who are now ministers studied the former "Timothy Plan" under him before passing their ministerial examinations.

Several of these new ministers planted churches in Brooklyn, Manhattan and Queens in New York Metro and even as far away as Florida. Reverend Jacques supported new missions financially and provided them with spiritual nurture as an experienced inner-city minister. His zeal for a well-trained clergy led him to initiate an Extension Bible Studies Program.

In 1992, Dr. Jacques was made chairman of the International Haitian Convention, a fellowship that meets every year with the Haitian constituency of the Church of God in North America.

More Outstanding Evangelists

Isaiah Campbell

Campbell was born in Jamaica. After his conversion he ministered there some before going to England, where he was to remain for 25 years. In his adopted country, he served three pastorates and planted two churches. He graduated from the Ebenezer Bible Institute and taught there for 16 years while serving as district overseer. In 1982 Campbell felt impressed to come to the Church of God Theological Seminary in Cleveland, Tennessee. He graduated in 1984 with the master of divinity degree and was appointed cross-cultural coordinator at the multicultural Ministerial Training Institute in Florida.

In Florida Campbell pioneered the Norwood Church of God, which started with 12 people and now averages about 200 members. Because of his involvement in education and church planting, he has already been involved in planting 14 congregations, many of them founded by former students of the Institute, which reports a current student body of 12. The ministry of Dr. Campbell is on the cutting edge of the church-planting business. As leader of a ministerial institute, he trains new trailblazers for the kingdom of God and promotes the witness of his denomination.

Alphonso Slaughter

Alphonso Slaughter was the first black national evangelist in the Church of God. He was saved in 1956 and born in a Church of God family. He entered the ministry in 1960 and worked as assistant pastor, and then as pastor for 10 years in New Jersey. He served as state youth and Christian education director for four years in New

Telling the Story

Jersey and then went on to pastor in Pennsylvania. In 1972 he accepted an appointment as missionary evangelist under the Evangelism and Home Missions Department. At the General Assembly in 1974, Slaughter was honored to become the first black national evangelist. As an evangelist with national stature, Slaughter was mandated by the Evangelism Department to identify good prospects and encourage black preachers to work under the umbrella of the Church of God. At that time in the Black Belt, the black work was dwindling because the laborers were few. Slaughter did a good job in pioneering evangelism on the national level.

Wallace J. Sibley

Dr. Wallace Sibley is now the state overseer of southern New England. Because of his multiple achievements, he has been listed in *Who's Who in Religion in America*.

Sibley received his bachelor of arts degree in English from Edward Waters College and his masters of education degree from Florida A & M University in Tallahassee, Florida. He did graduate work at the Luther Rice Seminary, which later awarded him a doctorate. He received the call to the ministry and became licensed in 1965. He has pastored in Valdosta and Saint Mary's, Georgia, and Daytona and Jacksonville, Florida. He served five years as state youth director of Florida. In 1978 the position of southeastern director of the black churches was created. Sibley was the first to fill this position. As evangelism director, he preached extensively in Mississippi, Alabama, North and South Carolina, North and South Georgia and Tennessee. After his stint as

More Outstanding Evangelists

evangelism director, he went to Florida as state overseer. As overseer he made major renovations and reported a significant increase in finances. Because of his evangelistic abilities, he was made a guest speaker at the General Assembly in 1986.

Isaac Brunson

Pastor Brunson has been pastoring in Seaford, Delaware, since 1980, and was seated on the Committee on Cross-Cultural Ministries in 1990.

He is from Sumter, South Carolina. After his conversion, he joined the Church of God, entered the ministry, was licensed in 1962 and ordained in 1969. He pastored in Buffalo, New York, Pittsburgh and Pennsylvania before moving to Delaware. He filled many positions in the church, such as district youth and Christian education director and district overseer. At the state level, Brunson has been councillor, member of the Boards of Evangelism and Home Missions, and youth and Christian education. Because of his achievements, he was granted an honorary doctorate from Clarksville School of Theology.

Robert Brookins

Robert Brookins has pastored in Reading, Pennsylvania, since 1979 and is the current director of the Northeast Regional Fellowship. He is presently a director of United Way and the Council for Chemical Abuse. He is also a member of the Black Ministries Board of Directors. He is doing a marvelous work in evangelism.

The Reading Church of God has developed an extended network of multiple ministries such as prison, shelter, nursing and tutoring. Though he had no role model in social ministry, Brookins was able to articulate a holistic ministry model from his reading of Matthew 25. This contributed to the expansion the kingdom of God. He ministers weekly to about 500 people in the community and was pleased to report the salvation of more than 5,000 people from the various ministries of his church. He considers the highlight of his ministry to be his involvement in soulwinning. His objective for the Northeast Fellowship is to see it become the "extended arm of Christ."

Nathaniel Spease

Reverend Spease pastors the Mount Calvary Church of God, a growing congregation in Pottstown, Pennsylvania. He is a former member of the Black Ministries Board and the Editorial and Publications Board of the Church of God Publishing House.

Reverend Spease was saved in 1967 and began attending the Reading Church of God in Pennsylvania. Early on, he showed signs of leadership and worked in the Sunday school department as superintendent. He also became involved in prison and street ministry and later served as associate pastor. He felt a call to the pastorate and started pioneering a work in Pottstown, Pennsylvania. On January 19, 1978, the Speases moved to Pottstown. For a little while, nothing happened. Puzzled by the fact that the town did not offer a lot of employment opportunities, he asked the Lord, "Why have you sent me to build a church in a town where everybody is leaving?" Reverend Spease received a message in tongues which stated that in six months, God would bring people in. On June 1978, the church was organized with eight people. Today, Mount Calvary lists more than 200 members.

Unlike the typical black church, Mount Calvary has a large number of men. Men came to church and got saved but went back into the streets. In order to retain them in the church, Pastor Spease had to organize a Bible study from midnight to sometimes 4 a.m. These meetings were scheduled until the men claimed deliverance from drug abuse. This is urban evangelism!

Mount Calvary has developed its own job employment program—Visions Temps Services—that has already organized 12 affiliates in seven states by 1996. This program has been successful in placing hundreds of people who had previously been on public assistance in jobs. The church is proactive in evangelistic outreach and has maintained a television and radio ministry. Reverend Spease is becoming well known for his urban program and spoke on "Evangelizing Urban America" at the 1996 Unity of the Spirit Conference, sponsored by the black ministers.

Frankie McDonald

Frankie McDonald was born in 1944 and labored in South Georgia where he served as state liaison for black affairs. He was made national evangelist in 1982, a position he held until he died in 1986 on his way to preach a revival in Maryland. He was an energetic speaker and is remembered for his classic sermon, "Everybody ought to know who Jesus is." It has been revealed that his earthly ministry greatly extended the kingdom of God.

- He preached 2,108 sermons.

- He led to Christ 1208 sinners.
- He reported 175 confessions of Holy Spirit baptism.
- He organized one church.

Reverend McDonald is still fondly remembered by those who knew him.

C. C. Pratt

C.C. Pratt was the first director of what is now called the Black Ministries Department. He was born on July 3, 1933, in the Bahamas and later moved to the states. He is a trained musician and studied at the International Training School and the Church of God Theological Seminary. Later, he was awarded an honorary doctor of divinity by Lee University. Today he pastors an urban congregation in Chattanooga, Tennessee.

Pratt was raised in a Christian family and was attracted early to the Pentecostal faith. While unsaved, he covenanted to be a Pentecostal if he ever were to become a Christian. He enjoyed the fervency of Pentecostal worship. After moving to Florida he attended services in a local church, where his heart was impressed with the sword of the Spirit. However, he never made his way to the altar during the invitation. During the altar call, he remained in his back seat praying that not a soul would go forward, so he would not be embarrassed for not going. During a Wednesday night service, he was fully persuaded to join the mourner's bench, registering himself as one more member in the church of Jesus Christ.

After being baptized, Pratt served his local church at several levels, and was later selected as district youth and

More Outstanding Evangelists

Christian education director. God chose to call him to the pulpit ministry, and he begged the Lord in modesty to let him first pastor the smallest congregation in Florida. That is exactly what happened. Pratt pastored first in Leesburg, which had five members, and served four other pastorates before being called to the overseership of the Florida-Cocoa region in 1978. While pastoring in Deerfield, he accepted the role of state evangelism director. When Dr. Sibley was assigned to Florida in 1982 as overseer, Dr. Pratt became the regional director of the black churches and remained in this position 10 years. As the first national director of Black Ministries, he strengthened the black outreach efforts across America.

Joseph Jackson

Joseph Jackson was born in Jamaica and migrated with his parents at an early age to Springfield, Massachusetts. He attended Westfield State College (B.S.), Yale Divinity School, (M.A.R), Harvard Graduate School of Education (C.A.S), and Wesley Theological Seminary, where he was awarded a doctorate in ministry.

Saved while in the States, Jackson did not plan to enter the ministry. He was taken aback by the plight of the ministers he knew. He wanted a more gratifying social status. Nevertheless, after much struggle he surrendered his life to the call of the Master, who needed him in the harvest. He served in the early phase of his ministry as district youth director and associate pastor. To further prepare himself, he chose to attend Yale University and challenged those who said this Ivy League institution would derail him from "spirituality." As a student at Yale, Jackson attended the Blue Hills Church of God in

Telling the Story

Hartford, Connecticut. Here he was mentored by the pastor of the church at that time, the late Peter C. Barrett. After graduating from Yale Divinity School, Jackson entered the Harvard Graduate School of Education where he taught as a teaching fellow.

Tired of being torn between secular work and ministry, Jackson accepted an offer from Lee University to serve as associate professor of religion and counselor of minority affairs. During the same time, he served as pastor of the Inman Street Church of God in Cleveland, Tennessee. In 1990, Jackson went to Maryland and assumed the pastorate of Harvest Temple Church of God. In 1992 he was called to lead the Black Ministries Department. He vigorously stressed the importance for black people to be informed about their heritage in the Church of God and was responsible for many initiatives in this regard. Jackson designed the 1993 Biennial Black Ministries Conference, which saw black leaders, both native and foreign, discuss the history of the black Church of God in this country and abroad. The theme of that conference was "Revisiting Our History, Continuing Our Heritage." The same year, he published his book, *Reclaiming Our Heritage: The Search for Black History in the Church of God*, which is an attempt among other things to encourage blacks to "search" for their roots in the Church of God.

To celebrate Black History month in 1994, the Black Ministries Department sponsored cultural rallies in various regions of the country. The late H.G. Poitier, a former prominent leader, was the focal person during that period of commemoration. To better inform the black constituency about their heritage, this director of Black Ministries authored a series of articles on the leading figures of the black church, which were original in revealing information about the early history of blacks in Florida. Concurrently with his work in Cleveland, Jackson also served as secretary treasurer of the Northeast Regional Fellowship, and treasurer of the National Association of Evangelicals (1995-1998) and program director for the 1996 NAE convention. To promote church growth in the black church, he convened the Pace Setter Conference in July 1997. The following year, he resigned the directorship of Black Ministries to accept the pastorate of Blue Hills Church of God in Hartford, Connecticut, where he served until the end of Spring 1999.

Asbury R. Sellers

Asbury Sellers is the current director of Black Ministries. He was born to a devoted couple, Nathan and Gertrude Sellers. His mother was an evangelist who preached numerous revivals and planted several churches. In his early years, the young Sellers attended the Mount Harmon Church of God and was called to the ministry at the age of 17. His first pastorate was in Columbia, South Carolina, which he left to plant the Capitol Church of God in Washington D.C. Later, he was instrumental in planting eight churches in the same area.

He received his ministerial training at the Philadelphia Bible School, Lee University and the Church of God Theological Seminary. He was later awarded a doctoral degree by the Institute of International Studies.

One of the highlights of his ministry was to be a founding member of the Northeast Regional Fellowship in 1978. In 1986 he replaced Frankie McDonald as national evangelist and traveled widely, preaching the gospel in more than 50 countries. In 1994 he was the pioneer for the Southeast Regional Fellowship, which has met every year since. At the 1994 General Assembly, he was assigned to New Jersey as state overseer. He planted seven churches as state overseer and left New Jersey when he was asked to assume the directorship of Black Ministries in 1998. At the last General Assembly, his wife, Leola Sellers, was appointed to the national board of Women's Ministries. The threefold emphasis of Black Ministries under Bishop Sellers is: "Remembering our past, serving the present with honor and integrity, and reaching the future."[3]

Quan L. Miller

Reverend Quan L. Miller has been the overseer of Florida-Cocoa since 1990 and is the offspring of a family with a long history in the Church of God. He is related to Zora Miller, his aunt, and to Emily Miller, his mother, both of whom were trailblazers in the early years of the black Church of God.

Dr. Miller is a native of Florida and graduated from Lee University with a degree in elementary and Christian education. He received further schooling at the Luther Rice Seminary in Jacksonville, Florida. He pastored in Stuart, Fernandina and Deerfield Beach, Florida. He served his denomination as Christian education director and as a member of the General Board of Education. Dr. Miller is the longest serving black state overseer in the modern history of the black Church of God and serves as an advisor to the Black Ministries Board and a member of the Lee University Board of Directors.

Under Dr. Miller, Florida-Cocoa acquired a 52-acre

More Outstanding Evangelists

campground for $1.5 million. This facility accommodates a chapel, a cafeteria, a motel, various cabins and a gymnasium that seats 3,000 people. This region, which was long considered to be primarily an African-American bulwark, has become more multicultural, welcoming all kinds of ethnic groups. Reverend Miller identifies this current mood in this well-meaning statement.

> We don't see ourselves as an exclusively African-American church anymore . . . we are striving for ethnic and cultural diversity. Many of our churches are racially and ethnically mixed. We have congregations that are primarily Hispanic, primarily Jamaican, and primarily Haitian. We want to be a church for all people.[4]

Chapter 10

Social Ministry and Education

The area of social ministry is one which is frequently overlooked but is a great asset to any church. Here we will look at some of the black men and women in the Church of God who contributed to this ministry.

Marion Spellman

Marion Pegues was born in 1943 and raised in Pennsylvania. Coming from a Baptist background, she attended a Pentecostal revival and later joined the Church of God in Pittsburgh, where E. D. Cobbs was pastor. While in Pittsburgh, she worked for the Allegheny County Prisons and developed familiarity with the incarcerated women in that area. At first she was unsure about her readiness and capacity to minister within the penitentiary system, but while praying, she felt impressed to circle seven times the prison where she was to minister. She obeyed the leading of the Holy Spirit and her ministry continued.

This burden for these desperate women led her to minister to them and later to invite them to her church. Unfortunately, while her pastor was very

Telling the Story

much appreciative of her efforts, the congregation was at loss on how to deal with people coming from behind bars. This reaction lit the first spark for what Marion would later do in life.

Marion moved to Harrisburg and secured a job at the Bureau of Corrections, working for the Commissioner's Office. In this office she gained valuable experience that would be helpful when the time came for her to affirm her ministry. While living in Harrisburg, Marion was tremendously saddened by the helplessness of her mother, who did not know how deal with a relative who was addicted to drugs. Moved by this, Marion made a vow to God to be instrumental in providing relief to other mothers facing similar situations and entered the area of social ministry. She resigned from her job and became involved with Teen Challenge. It was there that she met and married Harold Spellman.

In the early '80s, Dr. Spellman miraculously secured a place outside of Harrisburg to open a ministry for those who were abusing drugs and alcohol. With little money of her own, she was able to raise $7,000 in one week after being pressed for $1,500 in order to occupy a place to conduct her ministry. The Lord provided the money and Peniel Ministry was born.

Today Dr. Marion Spellman and her husband are leaders of this drug and alcohol rehabilitation program which has assisted thousands of addicted people. They offer a variety of services. Because of their faith, the Spellmans have provided a Christian approach to what could have been only a secular institution. They are impressed that many of their clients have met the Lord and are now in a position to take care of themselves and their families. More than 5,000 clients have been treated in almost two decades and two Peniel extensions have opened in Michigan and South Africa. Marion and Harold Spellman have been two distinguished honorees. Marion Spellman was the recipient of the National Association of Evangelicals' Award for "High Commitment to Social Concern in Evangelism." In 1996 the mayor of Johnstown, the city where Peniel is located, declared November 3, 1996, "Drs. Harold and Marion Spellman Appreciation Day." An official proclamation encouraged all residents to be inspired by the Spellmans' love of mankind. Because of her dynamic leadership, Dr. Spellman was appointed to the National Board of Women's Ministries in 1990.

Jesse E.C. Abbott

Reverend Jesse E.C. Abbott is the pastor of The Family Worship Center in Salisbury, Maryland. He has been a member of the Board of Directors of the Church of God Theological Seminary since 1992. He was educated at Delaware University, where he received a degree in mathematics.

Reverend Abbott was saved in the Methodist Church and joined the Church of God through the influence of his in-laws. He first attended the Seaford Church of God, pastored by the late E.D. Cobbs, whom he was privileged to have as a mentor. When he received a call to his first and only pastorate in 1974, he was reluctant at first, knowing that he had no prior pastoral experience. Nevertheless, he accepted the challenge and assumed the leadership of a congregation with three people. The Lord blessed Reverend Abbott's ministry through community involvement and street preaching, and he has been able to win many souls to the kingdom of God. In the early years, he was a bivocational minister but later was asked by God to relinquish a secure teaching position at a secular institution in order to work full-time in the ministry. His congregation has grown from modest beginnings and claims today a membership of more than 300.

One of Reverend Abbott's significant contributions was attracting foreign-born blacks to participate in the Northeast Regional Fellowship while he served as president of this great body from 1984-1988. Currently, he is the vice president of this Fellowship.

Ridley Usherwood

Dr. Ridley Usherwood is the director of intercultural studies at Lee University and pastors in Charleston, Tennessee. He is also a reserve chaplain in the Air Force with the rank of lieutenant colonel. As such, he teaches to hundreds of military personnel every summer in areas such as world religions, multicultural diversity and ethical boundaries.

Usherwood was born in Jamaica and migrated to England. He graduated from Handsworth Technical College in England with a concentration in pre-medical and nursing studies. Then he migrated to Switzerland in order to enroll at the European Bible Seminary. After majoring in pastoral studies, he graduated with a diploma in theology in 1965 and returned to England to teach at the Ebenezer Bible Institute. He came to the United

Social Ministry and Education

States in 1968 in order to attend Lee University. Following his graduation from Lee in 1970, he matriculated in the master of divinity program at Gordon-Conwell Theological Seminary in Massachusetts. From Gordon-Conwell, Usherwood went on to Rudersberg, Germany, to assist Heinrich Scherz in reorganizing the European Bible Seminary.

In the land of the Great Reformer, Usherwood was tenured as academic dean and registrar. Fluent in German, he studied church history and theology at the famous University of Tubingen. In 1980 Usherwood became visiting professor of World Missions at the Church of God Theological Seminary and later moved to England to help organize Overstone Bible College in Northampton. Serving as president, he was responsible for securing accreditation for the new college. In England, Usherwood was honored with many distinctions. He served on the Board of Education of both the British Council of Churches and the Evangelical Alliance.

In 1991, Usherwood returned to Lee University to teach. After years of post-graduate studies at the Oxford Center for the Study of Missions, he finally secured his doctorate in ministry degree from Columbia Theological Seminary in Decatur, Georgia in 1994. Dr. Usherwood is now finishing his dissertation for the Ph.D. to be conferred by the University of Birmingham, England.

One of the highlights of his ministry is networking with a diversity of people and serving in the area of practical ministry. As an Air Force chaplain, he has been privileged to lecture to a worldwide audience through "distance learning" electronic programs.

Education

In the area of education, blacks opened up the educational school of the Pentecostal Movement. In 1912 Fuller organized the William Fuller Normal Industrial Institute in Atlanta, Georgia. In 1932 Bishop John Curry, a black bishop of the Church of God, boldly recommended to the Bishops' Council the immediate organization of a theological seminary. This would have been the first such institution created after Azusa Street in a Pentecostal denomination. Curry was ahead of his time. His dream was to be realized by Bishop J.O. Patterson (Church of God in Christ), a son-in-law of Charles Mason. Patterson inaugurated the Charles H. Mason Theological Seminary in 1970, the first seminary ever organized in the entire Pentecostal world. Black Pentecostals who have received graduate degrees in the field of religion are now teaching in a wide spectrum of institutions.

- David Daniels (Church of God in Christ), McCormick Theological Seminary;

- Alonzo Johnson (Church of God in Christ), University of South Carolina;

- Trevor Grizzle (Church of God), Oral Roberts University;

- Avril Livingstone (Church of God), Colgate Rochester Divinity School);

- Estrelda Alexander, Wesley Theological Seminary;

- William Turner (Original United Holy Church), Duke University Divinity School;

Social Ministry and Education

- Leonard Lovett (Church of God in Christ), Regents University School of Divinity;
- James Forbes (Original United Holy Church of America), Auburn Theological Seminary.

Dr. Forbes, called "the preacher's preacher," is especially noted for his superb preaching skills, and was the Harry Emerson Fosdick adjunct professor of preaching at Union Theological Seminary. He was called to be the first Luce Lecturer at the Harvard Divinity School. Robert Franklin, affiliated with Church of God in Christ, is the current president of the Interdenominational Theological Center in Atlanta, Georgia, a consortium of several black seminaries.

A few years ago, the late Bishop Ithiel Clemmons served as president of the Society for Pentecostal Studies and chairman of the Pentecostal and Charismatic Churches of North America. At the last meeting of this academic society, Sherry DuPree (Church of God in Christ) was elected first vice president of this international Pentecostal forum.

Bishop Barbara Amos, a black woman preacher from the United Holy Church of America has recently been seated as the co-chairperson of the Pentecostal and Charismatic Churches of North America. She currently pastors Faith Deliverance Christian Center, a 3,000-member congregation in Norfolk, Virginia. Bishop Amos and Sherry Dupree are certainly some of the highest ranking black women leaders involved in interchurch relations and academia within Pentecostal circles.

Chapter 11

Missions in the Black Church

The success in the mission field has made the black church what it is today. This chapter will look at some the ministers who have worked in the harvest fields of Africa, Asia and Europe spreading the good news.

Selwyn Arnold

Dr. Selwyn Arnold, state overseer of New Jersey, has worked in the Church of God in several capacities. The Arnolds served on the mission field for more than 20 years. Their story as a couple is perhaps unique in the Church of God.

Selwyn Arnold was born in Tobago on May 29, 1934. At an early age, he involved himself in scouting and excelled at that so much that he represented his country at an international jamboree in Jamaica. After hearing a sermon on the miracle of the blind man, he surrendered his life to Christ and started attending the Pilgrim Methodist Church. While attending a revival in neighboring Trinidad, he received the Baptism of the Holy Spirit and entered the ministry. Pursuing his schooling, he studied public health and worked in this field for a while. He also became licensed and served his first pastorate.

In 1957 he moved to England where he attended the Stoke Newington Church. There, he worked with the local missions board until he was called to be the first national youth director of England in 1960. In this position he worked with his overseer, Reverend Oliver Lyseight, to establish the Ebenezer Bible Institute. In his new homeland, he met his future wife, Joyce, whom he married in 1963. She was to be one of the first students of the Bible School.

While working diligently for the expansion of the Youth Department, the Arnolds were appointed by World Missions to be missionaries to Ghana in 1966.

After some soul-searching, these West Indians took a long journey to the continent of their ancestors, certainly not knowing what would be next. The situation in Ghana was bleak: there were only five pastors, no property and a debt of $800. In other words, they had to start from almost nothing. One year after their arrival, the Arnolds opened a local Bible school in their rented house with seven students.

Ministering in Africa was more than lecturing in a four-walled building: it also involved engaging in spiritual warfare. The Arnolds felt confident about their God and launched a crusade in a city that was filled with witches. While doing ministerial work, their van inexplicably overturned. The demons were real. Nevertheless, many people were saved and healed.

One of the peculiarities of the Arnolds' missionary work was their involvement in physical caretaking.

Missions in the Black Church

While in England, Mrs. Arnold was denied the opportunity to received her ministerial credentials on her own, and decided to complete her nursing studies. As a nurse, she was moved by the enormous physical plight of the Ghanaians. She rented a building in Essienimpong and turned it into a clinic. With the help of the churches of England, a full-fledged clinic was built and was operational by 1974. At the end of their term, the Church of God in Ghana had one Bible school and the value of their properties rose from $500 to over $72,000.

The Arnolds enrolled at Lee University in 1974 and graduated with honors. Reverend Arnold majored in Bible and historical studies and graduated summa cum laude. His wife majored in Christian education and also graduated with honors. After the completion of their studies, they were appointed to Nigeria.

In their personal reminiscences, they must have recalled that they both had been foretold, separately, that they would serve the Lord in Africa. While a young convert, Selwyn was shown by the Lord that he would minister in a land with many rivers and forests. At the age of 17, young Joyce was told under a mango tree that she will be a missionary in the continent of Ham.

The Arnolds went to Nigeria and received God's approval on their Nigerian ministry. A young man, who was walking with crutches and believed to be demon-possessed, received deliverance. With this divine approval, the Arnolds regained their composure and went full-throttle in the Master's work.

Once again, they were called upon to relieve the sufferings of their constituency. Jesus did not only deal

Telling the Story

with spiritual problems, he also relieved the physical infirmities of fallen humanity. They could do no less than the Master. One evening, God commanded this overseer of Nigeria to build a clinic. With his wife trained as a nurse and midwife, it was fairly easy. The local people raised more than $11,000 towards this project. The clinic was built and was supervised by three Nigerian doctors. During the Nigerian ministry of the Arnolds, the worth of the properties rose from $61,055 to $810,006.

In the area of education, Selwyn Arnold contributed to the development of the youth program in Nigeria. In 1978 the first national youth director was hired. A native who studied in the United States helped improve the quality of Christian education in Nigeria. Continuing education was encouraged for the ministers and several enrolled in the External Studies Program of Lee University.

As they blessed others, the Arnolds were blessed in return. In 1979 Mrs. Arnold, who had been instrumental in the delivery of other people's babies, was blessed with a child—Selwyn Arnold Jr.

After more than seven years of ministry in Nigeria, the Arnolds returned to the United States in 1984. Reverend Arnold received his M.A. at the Church of God Theological Seminary and was later awarded the doctor of ministry degree by Sheffield University, England. He was reassigned to England in 1984 where he served as overseer for eight years.

Curtis Grey

Curtis Grey, a regional superintendent in Africa, was born April 3, 1934, in Jamaica. He was saved in 1952 and called to preach at the age of 20. He immigrated to

Missions in the Black Church

England, where he married his first wife, Phoebe, in 1958. He pastored for 15 years in Leeds and evangelized extensively in Bradford, Huddersfield, Halifax, Workshop and Chesterfield. After he and a fellow minister preached a two-week campaign in Cardiff, Wales, a Church of God was established in that region for the first time. He served on the national council and on the school board nine years. He studied at Birmingham Bible Institute and London University, and was later awarded the doctor of ministry degree from International Seminary in Florida.

Curtis Grey was appointed to Liberia in 1973 and moved there in 1974. The Church of God became interested in Liberia after Lyseight, national overseer of England, visited to that country.

Grey was responsible for setting in order the first Church of God in Liberia and ultimately founded a Bible school. The school opened on March 2, 1977, with six students. For some time, Reverend Grey remained the principal teacher due to the lack of native personnel. Because of his determination to win Africa for God, Grey could report 10 missions, 1,525 members and one Bible school by 1979. This same year, his wife died of malaria. Sadly, Grey had to return to England for a funeral on a snowy day. At the funeral, the officiating minister, Reverend Jeremiah McIntyre, commented on the devotional life of Grey. While this missionary was praying and fasting for revival in Africa, he heard a voice that asked him: "Would you give your wife for revival in Africa?" Grey answered, "I don't know."

In His sovereignty, God chose to remove Phoebe Grey to a higher sphere, and Grey went through the trial. After the funeral, he said "I will be going back within a few weeks." He remained there for another five years and left Liberia in 1980.

In 1984 Grey went to Nigeria, and organized six new churches within one year. He was no novice having done church planting work both in England, North Carolina and Liberia.

Andre Marcelin

Andre Marcelin was born in Haiti into a Catholic family with aspirations to enter the priesthood. After graduating from high school, he entered a Catholic seminary managed by the Oblates of Mary Immaculate, where he remained for three years.

One summer he spent time with one of his cousins, whom he tried to convert to the Catholic faith. This particular cousin was a member of the Church of God and staunchly defended the doctrines of her church. Challenged with Biblical arguments by his Protestant relative, Andre cornered a Belgian priest and begged him for answers. The priest was taken unawares and could only tell the young man to ignore these "people." Marcelin was disappointed. Once while swimming, he reached deep waters and lost contact with the outside world. Then, in a Jonah-like experience, he heard a Protestant melody. Puzzled, he came out of the water and found nobody singing at the shore. He then started to act in an uncommon way, which led his Catholic friends to mock him by saying that he was acting like a Protestant. Marcelin surrendered his life to Christ that same night and received a call to the Christian ministry.

Missions in the Black Church

This was about the time that the Church of God Bible School was opening in Haiti. He enrolled in this Pentecostal institution where he would meet his future wife, Andree Manoli. After three years, Andre Marcelin graduated and went to his hometown to assist the local pastor. By then he was credentialed in the Church of God.

When the Petersons were sent to Haiti in 1963, Marcelin was offered a teaching position at the Bible school. Concurrently with teaching, he maintained a pulpit ministry. In 1974 he was made education director and led the Bible school for three years. This was a time when there were few French documents available, and the Marcelins painstakingly had to translate numerous English texts in French for instructional purposes. Their ministry at the Bible school allowed then to train scores of ministers, many of whom are now pastoring in the United States and Canada.

While devoutly serving the Lord, Pastor Marcelin dreamed and saw himself dressed as an African chief. He did not understand what was going on. For years, Pastor Marcelin had been taking offerings in his local congregation and would ask the Missions Board to send them to Africa. He nurtured such a burden for Africa, he named his last son Livingstone in remembrance of the great missionary. His prayers were that the Lord would call his son as a missionary to the African people.

In 1977 the Church of God was looking for a French-speaking missionary to go to Africa, and appointed the Marcelins to go to Chad to do ground-breaking work. Pastor Marcelin and his family packed up and left their cherished homeland for the old continent.

Telling the Story

In Chad the Marcelins were expected to establish a ministerial training program. This was not new for them, since they had spent all their lives training ministers. In the beginning, they held Bible studies twice each week and rallied as many people as they could around them. Their plan was to train Sunday school teachers who would train others. Because of the non-availability of French documents, they had to prepare the lessons themselves. The most educated natives were made teachers. They, in turn, translated the instructional materials in the languages of the people. In the church at N'Djamena alone there were four different languages spoken.

The labors of these committed workers were cut short in 1980 by internecine wars, which forced them to leave the country. Reverend Marcelin spared his life by passing for dead. At the General Assembly of 1980, Reverend Marcelin was reassigned to Haiti as superintendent. He served in this capacity until 1991, when he moved to the United States. He has since been pastoring in Seaford, Delaware. He is the only Haitian national to have served as a missionary in Africa. Reverend Eugene Germain, endorsed by World Missions, served in Guadeloupe for six years (1968-1974).

Avril Livingstone

Avril Livingstone was born in Trelawny, Jamaica, and made the classic journey to England with her family. She reached the United Kingdom in the early '50s at the age of 9 and was saved in July 1967 in a Church of God service. Baptized in the Holy Spirit in 1970, she felt called to missionary work. Nevertheless, she went on to study biochemistry at Paddington and Goldsmith in England.

While working in medical technology, she decided to enroll at the European Bible Seminary in Germany. Upon graduation, she entered the ministry in England.

Back in the United Kingdom, Livingstone acted in several capacities. She pastored, evangelized, taught at Ebenezer Bible Institute and became a youth director for the Balsath District of Birmingham. But the time for her missionary service was approaching. Livingstone was appointed in 1979 as an instructor-missionary to Liberia by the New Testament Church of God in England. Six years later, she assumed the position of educational director.

In Liberia, Livingstone, a single woman, pastored and led the youth program. In 1982 she organized the first National Youth Convention of the Church of God in Liberia. While in Africa, Livingstone also worked with the Pentecostal Union of Africa. She later moved to America in order to further her education. She now holds two masters degrees: masters of divinity at the Church of God Theological Seminary and a masters of theology at the Princeton Theological Seminary. She is a candidate for the Ph.D. in Patristics at St. Louis University and teaches at Colgate Rochester Divinity School, New York, as an instructor in historical theology and black church studies.

Charles Harris

Charles Harris was the first black missionary to be appointed to Haiti. His story began in 1976 as a second-year medical student at Howard University. He was saved through the influence of his brother, Terry, who had surrendered his life to the Lord. After graduation from medical school, he joined the army and worked as a surgeon before finally landing in the Pentagon. He also served in many states, including Hawaii, where God called him to missions. Because of the strength of this conviction, he resigned his commission to further his interests in missions. In 1981 Harris was deeply moved by the death of one of his friends. Shattered by this unfortunate event, Harris begged God to raise another minister to replace him. He was told that he would be the replacement.

To gain more self-confidence in his call, the Reverend Harris and his wife, Karen, visited Haiti twice and received there divine confirmation that Haiti was to be their field of missionary work. Reverend Harris was blessed to have a companion devoted to the same cause. Several of her statements are indicative of her staunch commitment to further the kingdom of God in this Caribbean nation. Talking about her call to Haiti, Karen Harris declared: "We're simply being obedient to God and doing what God has called us to do. We have found the joy, happiness and peace that attend the Christian life through giving ourselves fully to our Lord and to His call."

It was hard for them to leave an affluent situation to go to an underdeveloped country. But there was faith. "There's nothing," said Mrs. Harris, "we can give up that God will not bless us and give back a hundredfold. We will get our reward, if not in this life, in the life to come."

The Harrises have contributed in many ways to relieve pain among the Haitians. Blessed with a nurse-wife, Dr. Harris has not only worked in the Church of God settings, but he has also assisted local orphanages in medical care. One of the highlights of his ministry was to have gone to the Dominican Republic and worked through the Christian Medical Society, ministering to the physical and spiritual needs of Haitian cane field workers. He is now on furlough in the States.

Horace Spragg

Horace Spragg is now a missionary in Zimbabwe and has been in Central Africa since 1990. He was born a Roman Catholic in Panama and was saved at the age of 21. Feeling a call to the Christian ministry, he enrolled at Zion Bible Institute in Providence, Rhode Island. After the completion of his training, he evangelized one year in the United States before returning to his homeland.

In Panama, Reverend Spragg pastored the church in Colon and filled the position of national youth director from 1961-62. While in the pastorate, he received a divine impression that he will serve in Africa. From 1965-1972, he worked in the Southwest as the leader of the black work in the Texas area. Afterwards, he returned to Panama to pastor for the next eight years. Then he served as national overseer. During a 10 year overseership, the Church of God in Panama underwent tremendous increase in membership (400 percent) and churches (100 percent). While serving as overseer, he became a member of the Panamanian Atlantic Religious Workers Association, the Pacific Workers Association, and CONELA (Latin-American Evangelical Fellowship).

At the 1990 General Assembly, Spragg was assigned as superintendent of Northern and Central Africa. He was the first black to be a high-ranking official in World Missions and worked in this capacity for six years. He is

Telling the Story

remembered in Africa as an advocate for Christian discipleship. In fact, he started discipling as early as three months after his arrival.

Chapter 12

The Modern Period 1967-Present

In the modern period, blacks have been concerned about the issues of ministerial training, ethnic fellowship and representation.

Early on, blacks in the Church of God discussed ways by which their ministers could further their theological training. Bishop Curry even talked about opening a theological seminary in the '30s. Several local Bible classes were taught, but it was felt that these were not enough. Many ministers were frustrated because they could not attend the denominational school, Lee College (Lee did not admit native blacks at that time).

Many ministers enrolled through the Bible Correspondence Program, but they wanted more. J.T. Roberts pushed for the organization of a Bible school, and in 1971 the denomination established the mobile Florida Bible Institute. Visiting ministers taught practicums for six weeks in Florida, and contributed to upgrading the educational level of the ministry. At the time of its inception, the Florida Bible Institute Committee was composed of: H.G. Poitier, chairman; Peter Hickson, secretary-treasurer; Thomas Chenault

Telling the Story

and Leon Deveaux. The current leaders of the Black Ministries Department, Wallace Sibley and Asbury Sellers, organize workshops/seminars at the regional levels and provide qualified students with scholarships, which allows more young black preachers to enter the denomination's schools of higher learning. It is understood that without the ongoing training of more black clergy, the black harvest will be seriously handicapped.

In the aftermath of the process of integration, the annual black assembly was eliminated, so the main vehicle for black fellowship was eliminated. Sensing a need for ethnic fellowship, Ruth Adams, a young black choir leader and evangelist, organized a black choir in 1978 to sing at the assembly. This was the nucleus for something bigger. In 1979 Dr. Samuel Ellis, a young minister, gathered 150-250 people in Reading, Pennsylvania for what was called the Sixth-State Fellowship — a meeting of black delegates from six states. Today this small gathering has evolved into the celebrated Northeast Regional Fellowship, which meets every year with about 4,000 delegates in attendance. Reverend Robert Brookins is the current president of the Northeast Regional Fellowship.

In 1975 Willie Vaughn, director of metro ethnic affairs, brought to fruition the Northwest Pentecostal Fellowship, which is now led by Bishop Samuel Irving.

Today there are three other black fellowships: the Midwest Regional Fellowship with Dr. Joscelyn Williams (former missionary to Liberia) serving as president; the Del-Mar, DC Regional Fellowship with Reverends Jimmy Campbell and Hattie Stanley serving as presidents; and the Southeast Regional Fellowship with Bishop James

The Modern Period 1967-Present

Monroe as president. This southern fellowship was organized in 1994 by Dr. Asbury Sellers, the current director of Black Ministries. It unites the southeastern congregations, and meets every year with around 2,000 in attendance.

There is another conference that meets biennially. In 1983 Dr. C.C. Pratt, evangelism director of the black churches, started the first Regional Convention of the Black Churches in Atlanta, Georgia. There were 1,200 blacks from all over the world who joined for a great time of spiritual and cultural fellowship. In the words of a participant, that conference "brought our ethnic groups together into a common homogeneous group. Each was able to worship in his or her own way."[1] This convention has become a biennial national meeting and is an important event for all blacks to attend.

The other concern of black constituents in the Church of God has been the issue of representation. In the '50s and '60s, America experienced a major social revolution through the civil rights movement. This quest for equality impacted ecclesiastical structures, particularly those of the predominantly white denominations. In the '60s, the National Committee of Black Churchmen led several denominations to organize black interest groups. Consequently, blacks in white churches increasingly became more vocal about the urgency to have full integration in the aftermath of the passage of the Civil Rights Act of 1964. In the '70s, state associations in the Southern Baptist Convention elected several black presidents and vice presidents. In 1971, the American Baptist Churches, USA, was able to elect its first black president, Thomas Kilgore.

Telling the Story

Blacks in the Church of God were people of their times who re-energized the struggle for inclusiveness in the church in the '70s. A review of the literature indicates that ministers from the South were among those who were the least reserved about what they wanted to see happen. This may be attributed to the fact that they experienced the struggles of the civil rights movement to a greater extent than those who were in New England or in the Midwest.

In the '70s, the *Church of God Evangel* ran several articles expressing the deep concerns of the black constituency for an integrated church. In 1971 Randle Witcher from Roanoke, Virginia, stated to Hollis Green, director of public relations, "I think that we should have some representation in all departments of our church. Some appointments might be made specifically to alleviate this problem."[2] In the same interview, Alphonso Menendez, a southern preacher who was pastoring in Freehold, New Jersey, responded to Heinrich Scherz, administrative editor of the *Church of God Evangel*. "A lot of wisdom has to go into our dealings with one another. Things are not going to change overnight. I do believe that we have qualified men — black men — who could hold any position in the church."[3] During the mid-'70s, more protests continued to be aired in favor of black representation. Finally in 1974, Alphonso Slaughter was appointed as the first black national evangelist. Four years later Wallace Sibley, who was pastoring in south Georgia became the first incumbent of the newly created position of southeastern regional director of evangelism.

The Modern Period 1967-Present

It was more difficult for blacks at the state level to be included in leadership, partly because of the congregational nature of the polity of the church. In order to be elected state councillor, a minister must receive the highest number of votes. In states where there were few black churches, black ministers just could not be elected. This was even more complicated in those areas where black pastors had not been ordained—they just would not be eligible to vote. A corollary in this is that it has been difficult for blacks in some parts of the Black Belt to become members of state councils. Though integration was made official in 1966, it was not until 1984 that a black minister, Jimmy Campbell, was privileged to be seated in the council of a black state that had more than 12 churches—South Georgia. This difficulty experienced in the South did not exist in the North, which carried a number of black churches by the end of the '80s. In New York Metro, black churches proliferated under Reverend Golden, and even foreign-born blacks, such as Honore Jacques and Peter Gayle, secured seats on the state council. In New Jersey, W.C. Menendez was elected to the state council.

In 1986 the polity of the church was revised and six more seats added to the Council of Twelve. Wallace Sibley and Goodwin Smith were elected to the Council of Eighteen at the General Assembly in 1986. Blacks had become more aware of the need to participate in the electoral process. This spirit of collegiality was certainly an outcome of the biennial regional rallies held by Dr. Pratt beginning in 1983.

The Church of God is also episcopal in its polity, allowing its leaders to be vested with many appointive powers.

Telling the Story

Unfortunately, this appointive privilege did not work in favor of the ethnic minorities. The record indicates that no blacks were appointed to any executive position at any level within the church (state and general) during the '60s, '70s and '80s. Aware of the complications associated with the church's electoral system, blacks became more focused and pressured the leadership to appoint blacks to visible executive positions—especially those areas that had a large black constituency. The '80s saw the changing of the guard—second- and third-generation constituents, who had honed their ministerial skills through college and university studies, become more assertive about their rights and educational achievements. Black leaders in the Church of God may have been influenced in the '80s by new developments on the religious scene. Blacks in other denominations, such as the American Baptist Churches, USA, and the United Methodist Church, were being rewarded with positions of leadership at the national level.

In any case, these biennial conferences became arenas where educated black ministers read and responded to papers, just as they would do in a formal academic setting. The phenomenal success of Reverend Golden in New York and California alerted the denomination to the need for black deployment, especially for evangelistic purposes. On the other hand, the principles of the Church Growth Movement of Donald McGavran and Peter Wagner were being disseminated within the denomination. In 1987, a major seminar was held at the Church of God Theological Seminary, during which Church of God missiologists, professors from Lee University and from

The Modern Period 1967-Present

the seminary, cross-cultural church planters and other denominational officials magnified the "Homogenous Unit" principle. Black speakers who spoke at the conference were: Jimmy Campbell, C.C. Pratt, Peter Gayle and Guy Notice. Little by little, general leaders started to acquiesce to the idea of more black appointments. In 1990 Dr. Lamar Vest, newly elected general overseer, expressed an openness toward multicultural representation in his inaugural address:

> I want to be part of a church that finds a way to include people of all races and ethnic backgrounds at every level of ministry—a church that respects and utilizes the gifts and energies of its women—a church that serves both its teenagers and its senior citizens with the same enthusiasm. I want to be part of a church which is an international church, not just in name, but in practice.[4]

During the episcopacy of Vest, the Executive Council passed a Resolution Against Racism, which was read by the general overseer at the 1991 Biennial Conference of Black Ministries in Charlotte, North Carolina.[5] At the same conference, Dr. Vest spoke in his keynote address of black history in the church. He reminded the delegates that a black man carried the cross for Jesus; that the man who led the Azusa Street revival in Los Angeles was a black man, William J. Seymour; that our first missionary was a black man, Edmond S. Barr, and that much of our music is rooted in the gospel tradition birthed by blacks.

In early 1992 Lamar Vest, in conjunction with the Executive Committee, appointed Dr. Martin Wright,

Telling the Story

a prominent pastor, as state overseer of Southern New England—an area where the Church of God is predominantly black. This was a landmark. He was the first black overseer of a mixed state. At the time of Wright's installation in office, the *Southern New England Reporter* noted:

> Dr. Wright has distinguished himself by serving the Church as pastor evangelist, district overseer, state evangelism board member, state council member, state representative of West Indian Ministries, and as member of the General Cross-Cultural Committee. Presently Dr. Wright is serving as Chairman of the Ad Hoc Committee for Black Ministries, and is a member of the Lee College Board of Directors.[6]

While applauding these efforts, blacks continued to fight for more integration. Robert White, who became general overseer in 1994, was instrumental in dramatically increasing the number of blacks in leadership positions in the mainland and overseas, as he worked closely with Dr. Joe E. Jackson to consolidate the gains of the black Church of God. A high number of ministers were appointed under White's tenure (1994-early 1996). They were: Canute Blake, superintendent of Eastern Canada, and the entire Canadian work; Asbury Sellers, overseer of New Jersey; Ishmael Charles, overseer of Tortola, Virgin Gorda, U.S. Virgin Islands, St. Martin and Anguilla; and William Lee, Jr., national evangelist.[7]

It is impossible to explain this increase in black representation in the Church of God without taking account of other developments occurring in the Pentecostal world,

The Modern Period 1967-Present

which influenced both the white and the black leaders of the Church of God. In 1994 Bishop Underwood, from the Pentecostal Holiness Church and Chairman of the Pentecostal Fellowship of North America, convened a meeting in Memphis, Tennessee. The purpose of the meeting was to end the racial exclusiveness of this inter-church group, which since its inception in 1948 had not cooperated with black churches. Blacks were not invited to participate in its inaugural meeting, while choirs and delegates from the Church of God in Christ were common fixtures of the Pentecostal World Conferences.

Leaders from mainstream Pentecostalism met in Memphis, Tennessee, in October 1994 and vowed to destroy the separateness between the white and black denominations. The white Pentecostal Fellowship of North America (PFNA) was dissolved. Replacing it was the integrated Pentecostal and Charismatic Churches of North America with Ithiel Clemmons, a late bishop of the Church of God Christ, elected chairman of its board of directors. Ray Hughes, first assistant general overseer, and Lamar Vest, former general overseer of the Church of God, read papers at the Memphis Conference.

In 1995 and 1996, blacks in the church organized two meetings on unity and reconciliation, which adopted a sophisticated format where papers and responses were read by those who would easily comprise a list of Who's Who in the Church of God. At those conferences, theologians from the Church of God Theological Seminary, Lee University and the Charles H. Mason Theological Seminary, black leaders from America, England and Belgium, sociologists from Lee University, and prominent preachers (Drs. Paul Walker and T.L. Lowery) reached the highest level of oratory. They discussed with scientific scholarship, theological acumen, and pastoral sensitivity on the need for inclusiveness in the Church of God. Black speakers at these two conferences held in Atlanta, Georgia, and Cleveland, Tennessee, were: Jesse Abbott, Samuel Ellis, Wallace Sibley, Joel Edwards, Quan Miller, Nathaniel Spease, Ridley Usherwood, Martin Mutyebele, Cecil Mullings, Jeremiah McIntyre, Kenneth Hill, Jonathan Ramsey and Estrelda Alexander.

At the last General Assembly, Drs. Joseph Jackson, Wallace Sibley and Goodwin Smith were elected to the Council of Eighteen. Fedlyn Beason, a former national overseer of Jamaica, was appointed field director of the Caribbean and Daniel Vassell became the first youth director of the Caribbean. In the area of education, blacks made some inroad: Canute Blake, chairman, International Bible College, Saskatchewan, Canada.

The Memphis Miracle, the advocacy of Jesse Abbott and that of the other leaders of the regional fellowships, the dynamism of Dr. Joe E. Jackson, the openness of Drs. White, McGuire, and Walker all contributed to the elevation of more blacks to executive positions.

While for the casual observer, these appointments may be just bureaucratic decisions, for African-Americans they are quite meaningful. They consider these achievements to be the results of the earlier years of advocacy originating from ministers from the South who experienced less than what they deserved. Recently, a minister from the South summed it up by saying: "Black Americans did not get where they are on flower beds of ease. We had to fight for everything."

Conclusion

Black Pentecostals have many things to appreciate about their journey in the Church of God. Their history is rich and even linked to the Azusa Street revival. Blacks entered the church the year that A.J. Tomlinson was made moderator, and shaped the future of this Pentecostal denomination. Another thing worth recalling is the rich heritage the pioneers have entrusted to the succeeding generations. A great deal of creativity was demonstrated in the founding of social and educational institutions needed to better minister to the constituency. Perhaps more than any other black leader in the history of the church, Bishop Curry stressed the need for black Pentecostals to acquire ministerial training.

Today, many black families remain loyal to the church. Many of the pioneers would be honored to know that their sons and daughters have followed them in the ministry in the Church of God. Women have contributed a great deal to the progress of the church. We have to remember their hard work in behalf of destitute children in Eustis, Florida. Last, in

Telling the Story

the areas of evangelism, education and leadership, blacks have been notable players in the life of the denomination.

On the other hand, the general church has promoted the evangelistic thrust of the black church. T.L. Lowery, J.D. Golden and Billy Rayburn have vigorously promoted black outreach in the inner cities. They and others are to be credited for the current strength of the black work. In the '70s, many gifted black preachers challenged other blacks to reach out to their own.

The history of blacks is the church has been one of struggles and victories. They entered the church at the time that race relations were at their worst in the United States, especially in the South. Christian denominations, unfortunately, reflected southern mores in their governmental structures. Though members, the blacks could not enjoy all the benefits of spiritual equality in Christ. Through continuous advocacy, fueled by developments such as the civil rights movement and the emergence of liberal middle class young leaders, blacks have been able to more effectively contribute their evangelistic, administrative and educational abilities to the church at large. It was not easy.

On the other hand, there was a spirit of confidence that in spite of all vicissitudes, the work of the Lord must be carried on. Commenting on the zeal of black preachers in those early days, Peter Hickson wrote in the *Minutes of the 30th Annual Assembly of the Church of God Colored Work:*

> With a great zeal to preach the Word, they went into the hedges and highways and declared the gospel of Christ. Great sacrifices were made to

Conclusion

> bring lost souls to Christ. The ministers walked for miles to conduct revivals. As the gospel began to spread, souls were sanctified and were filled with the Holy Ghost. Churches were organized and set in order. Those who believed were of one accord and of one heart. Truly those were happy days.[1]

On the eve of the next millennium, blacks must believe that the best days are ahead. At the last General Assembly, a significant number of black leaders were both appointed to important positions. Dr. Lamar Vest, Dr. Robert White, Dr. Dennis McGuire and Dr. Paul Walker, the current general overseer, have in the last decades of this century made the Church of God more representative by appointing more blacks to executive positions.

The future of the black Church of God will be brighter only if it can appreciate its history, muster its resources and thus contribute more to the kingdom of God!

Chronology of Important Events in the Black Church of God

1909 Edmond Barr was licensed, as the first black minister, and goes to the Bahamas to preach the gospel.
1912 Barr is ordained.
1915 Barr became overseer of the black churches of Florida.
1917 Barr was removed as overseer of Florida.
1918 Blacks were given the privilege to make presentations at general assemblies.
1922 Thomas Richardson became the next black overseer of Florida since the dismissal of Barr.
1923 The first Sunday school in Jupiter, Florida was organized.
1923 David LaFleur was elected national overseer (1923-1928).
1925 David LaFleur convened the First Annual Assembly of the Black Church of God.
1926 F.J. Lee, general overseer, organized black churches into a national judicatory with the privilege to elect their own general overseer.
1927 National overseers were relieved from pastoring while in office.
1928 Black ministers relinquished the right to elect their national overseer and asks the general overseer to resume this privilege.
1928 John H. Curry became national overseer (1928-1938).
1930 The northern and southern black churches were consolidated into one judicatory.

Telling the Story

1932 Bishop John H. Curry was elected to the Council of Twelve (1932-1938).
1932 First National Youth Convocation (YPE) convened in Jacksonville, Florida.
1934 Church of God Industrial School and Orphanage, Eustis, Florida, was dedicated.
1936 The partially completed Jacksonville Auditorium was dedicated.
1936 First issue of *The Church of God Gospel Herald*, the black paper, was published.
1938 Norbert S. Marcelle was elected national overseer (1938-1946).
1942 The debt was eliminated of the Jacksonville Auditorium by N.S. Marcelle.
1944 Blacks requested that their national overseer be selected at the annual colored conventions.
1946 Willie Ford was elected national overseer (1946-1950).
1948 The debt of the Industrial School and Orphanage was eliminated.
1950 George Wallace became national overseer, (1950-1954).
1952 Mrs. Shirley Wallace organized the National Black Ladies Ministries.
1954 The completed Jacksonville Auditorium was dedicated.
1954 Willie Ford was elected national overseer (1954-1958).
1954 The National Missions Department was organized.
1958 J.T. Roberts was elected (white) national overseer (1958-1965).

Chronology of Important Events

1964 The Church of God passed a "resolution on human rights."
1965 David L. Lemons was elected (white) national overseer (1965-1966).
1966 The Church of God was formally integrated, and "color distinctions" were eliminated in official records. Black work is consolidated at the general assembly, except in Florida and Mississippi.
1968 W.C. Menendez was made first metro evangelist.
1970 The black work in Mississippi was integrated.
1970 Celestine Poitier joined the National Board of Womens Ministries.
1972 Elisha Parris was elected to the General Youth and Christian Education Board.
1974 Alphonso Slaughter became the first black national evangelist.
1978 Seminar on Black Outreach was held in Cleveland, Tennessee.
1978 David Poitier joined Lee University Board of Directors.
1978 Wallace Sibley was elected regional director of evangelism (1978-1982).
1980 C.C. Pratt was made a member of the Editorial and Publications Board.
1982 Frankie McDonald was appointed black national evangelist.
1983 The National Office of Black Ministries was created with C.C. Pratt as the first director (1983-1992).
1983 The First National Black Ministries Conference was organized in Atlanta, Georgia.
1984 Jimmy Campbell was the first black elected to the state council of a black state, South Georgia.

Telling the Story

1986 Wallace Sibley and Goodwin Smith were the first blacks elected to the Council of Eighteen.

1986 Thomas Chenault became the first African-American to join the Cross-Cultural Committee.

1986 Asbury Sellers was appointed national evangelist.

1986 The *Black Women in Church: Historical Highlights and Profiles* was published by Mrs. Janet Spencer.

1986 Robert Ramsey was made a member of the Board of Media Ministries.

1990 Horace Spragg was the first black to become a missionary superintendent in North and Central Africa.

1990 Ridley Usherwood was appointed to the Chaplains Commission.

1990 Joseph Jackson was appointed to the Board of Directors of Church of God Theological Seminary.

1991 Resolution against racism was passed by the Executive Council.

1992 Martin Wright, the first overseer of a mixed state (Southern New England) became the first chairman of Black Ministries Board of Directors.

1992 Joseph Jackson was elected Director of Black Ministries, (1992-1998).

1993 *Reclaiming Our Heritage: The Search for Black History in the Church of God* was published.

1994 Asbury Sellers became first black overseer of New Jersey.

1994 Canute Blake was appointed superintendent of Eastern Canada.

1994 There was a celebration of black Church of God History.

Chronology of Important Events

1994 William Lee was appointed national evangelist.
1994 The white Pentecostal Fellowship of North America was dissolved and the integrated Pentecostal and Charismatic Churches of North America Memphis Miracle was organized.
1995 A conference was held on "Racial Reconciliation" in Atlanta, Georgia by prominent Church of God black ministers.
1996 Unity of the Spirit Conference convened in Cleveland, Tennessee, by black leaders.
1997 The Pace Setter Conference was organized for black churches.
1998 Fedlyn Beason became the first black superintendent of the Caribbean.
1998 Daniel Vassell was appointed coordinator of youth ministries for the Caribbean.
1998 Asbury Sellers became the director of Black Ministries.

Black Overseers of Florida

1915-1917	Edmond Barr
1922-1923	Thomas Richardson
1923-1928	David LaFleur
1928-1958	National Overseers of the Colored Work
1958-1965	F.B. Bell
1965-1970	Walter Jackson
1970-1974	H.G. Poitier
1974-1978	W.C. Menendez
1978-1982	C.C. Pratt
1982-1986	Wallace Sibley
1986-1990	Wardell Avant
1990-Present	Quan Miller

Notes

CHAPTER 2

[1] *Minutes of the 48th General Assembly of the Church of God*, pp. 193-194; *Minutes of the 21st General Assembly of the Church of God*, pp. 38-39; *Minutes of the 23rd General Assembly of the Church of God*, p. 32.

[2] Conn, *Like a Mighty Army*, Pathway Press, Cleveland, TN, 1996, p. 377.

[3] Conn, p. 378.

[4] *Minutes of 34th Annual Assembly of the Church of God Colored Work*, p. 66.

[5] *Minutes of the 39th Annual Assembly of the Church of God Colored Work*, p. 17.

[6] Carolyn Dirksen, "A History of Black Churches in the Church of God," *Church of God Evangel*, 28 February 1972, pp. 11-12; *Minutes of the 39th Annual Assembly of the Church of God Colored Work*, pp. 26-27.

CHAPTER 3

[1] Conn, *Like a Mighty Army*, Pathway Press, Cleveland, TN, 1996, p. 269.

[2] Wallace Sibley, "Hopes of a Black Minister," *Church of God Evangel*, 28 February 1972, p. 13; Janet Spencer, ed., *Black Women in the Church: Historical Highlights and Profiles*, Pittsburgh, PA, 1986, p. 100.

[3] Douglas Leroy, "Evangelizing the Black Community," *Church of God Evangel*, 23 December 1974, p. 11.

[4] T. L. Lowery, "Black Churches to Double in a Decade," *Church of God Evangel*, 11 August 1976, p. 5.

Telling the Story

CHAPTER 4

[1] *South Georgia Accent*, June 1979, p. 8; *Tennessee Tidings*, December 1978, p. 8.

[2] Sibley, "Black Churches of U.S. Origin," *Church of God Evangel*, 22 May 1978, p. 7.

CHAPTER 5

[1] Oliver A. Lyseight, "A Church Is Born," 1971, p. 2, Church of God/England File, H.B. Dixon Pentecostal Research Center, Lee University, Cleveland, TN.

[2] Douglas Leroy, "Seizing the Moment," *Church of God Evangel*, April 1998, p. 5; *InSpirit*, Fall 1997, p. 8.

[3] Lyseight, pp. 4-7.

CHAPTER 6

[1] O.W. Polen, "The Cross-Cultural Ministry of the Church of God," July 1983, p. 8.

[2] "Consultants Appointed," *The Cross-Cultural Communicator*, First Quarter 1991, p. 1.

[3] Golden, J.D., "The Director's Page," *The Cross-Cultural Communicator*, Third Quarter 1990, pp. 2, 7.

[4] Golden, p. 7.

CHAPTER 7

[1] O.W. Polen, "The East Flatbush Church of God," *Church of God Evangel*, January 1988, p. 28.

[2] Polen, p. 28.

[3] Polen, p. 27; Pastor Gayle retired in 1994.

[4] Polen, p. 27.

[5] Honore Jacques, "Black Churches of Non-U.S. Origins," *Church of God Evangel*, 22 May 1978, p. 9.

Notes

[6] Othon Noel, "Winning My Haitian People," *The Pentecostal Minister*, Fall 1984, pp. 16-17.

[7] O.W. Polen, "They Kept the Church Doors Open," *Evangel*, 14 September 1981, p. 14.

[8] E.L. Cushman, Florida State News, March-April 1992, pg 6.

CHAPTER 8

[1] *Minutes of the Eighth Annual Assembly of the Church of God Colored Work*, pp. 8-9.

[2] *Minutes of the 30th Annual Assembly of the Church of God Colored Work*, p. 33.

[3] Dorothy Leek, "I Never Learned to Take No for An Answer," *Church of God Evangel*, 3 March 1979, p. 25.

[4] Oliver A. Lyseight, "A Church Is Born," 1971, p. 2, Church of God/England File, H.B. Dixon Pentecostal Research Center, Lee University, Cleveland, TN, p. 3.

[5] Dorothy Leek, p. 25; "Veteran Churchman Honored by Lee College," *SOW*, Fall 1995, p. 16; "Interview with Rev. O.A. Lyseight," *Vision*, January 1979, p. 15.

CHAPTER 9

[1] Russell Brinson, "A First for the Church of God: A Director of Metro Affairs," *Church of God Evangel*, 26 May 1975, p. 20.

[2] Interview of Rev. Willie Vaughn by author, 21 December 1998.

[3] "Meet the New Black Ministries Director's Page," Ebenezer, April-June 1998, p. 6; Interview of Bishop Sellers by author, 19 December 1998.

Telling the Story

[4] Marcus V. Hand, "The Church of God in Florida, Cocoa Conference," *Church of God Evangel,* August 1997, p. 23; Jackson, "Profiles in Black Leadership: Quan L. Miller," *Church of God Evangel,* July 1995, p. 11; Spencer, pp. 29-30.

CHAPTER 12

[1] "Convention Calls Blacks to Commitment," *Church of God Evangel,* 11 November 1983, pp. 14-15.

[2] "Negro Ministers Speak About Their Church and Ministry," *Church of God Evangel,* 24 June 1971, p. 20.

[3] "Negro Ministers Speak About Their Church and Ministry," p. 20.

[4] *Minutes of the 63rd General Assembly of the Church of God,* p. 58.

[5] "Resolution on Racism," *Church of God Evangel,* 15 October 1991, p. 13.

[6] "L. Martin Wright, New State Overseer of Southern New England," *Southern New England Reporter,* April 1992, p. 2.

[7] Interview with Dr. Joseph Jackson by author, 2 June 1999.

CONCLUSION

[1] *Minutes of the 30th Annual Assembly* of the Church of God Colored Work, p. 12.